UNITY LIBRARY 8 ARCHIVES
Hypnotism revealed: the Powers

T5-AGS-254

INDUCING HYPNOSIS BY THE CRYSTAL BALL TECHNIQUE

Here we see the correct sitting position for the induction of hypnosis. Note that the feet are placed squarely on the floor and that the hands are placed palms down on the lap. The hypnotist is using the Powers' hypnotic crystal ball as an object of concentration.

EYE TEST

The subject has been hypnotized. The challenge has been given that she will be unable to open her eyes until the hypnotist tells her to do so. She attempts to open them, but cannot. This is the first test to determine whether or not a subject is under hypnosis.

HAND TEST

After telling the subject to fold her hands, she has been instructed that she will be unable to break the hold no matter how vigorously she tries until directed to do so. Please note the strained condition of the hands as the subject futilely attempts to unlock them.

ARM TEST

The subject has been instructed to extend her arm. She has been further told that she will be unable to bend or lower it until given the command. The reader will note the upward curved extension of the fingers and further observe how the thumb is separated from the rest of the hand.

ROLLING HAND TEST

The subject, now wide awake, is performing a post-hypnotic suggestion. While under hypnosis, she had been told that when she hears her name mentioned upon awakening, she will have an uncontrollable desire to rotate her hands. This behavior was to contiune until terminated by the hypnotist. The subject found herself puzzled by this dilemma as she had no memory of having received such a post-hypnotic suggestion. It is apparent therefore that she had been in the somnambulistic state which as we know is the deepest state of hypnosis.

MATCH TEST

The subject has again been placed in the somnambulistic state and has been given the suggestion that since her right hand is numb she will be unable to feel pain. Note the complete lack of reflexive action as the lighted match is held under her palm.

AMMONIA TEST

A post-hypnotic suggestion has been given to the subject that upon awakening she would see a bottle of French perfume, pick it up, and smell its intriguing aroma. We see her carrying out this suggestion. The hypnotist having created the illusion has also altered her sense of smell. Even though the subject was inhaling full strength ammonia, she was as pleased as though she was sensing the lush fragrance of a heavy perfume. This test is an excellent one to determine both the depth and reality of the hypnotic state.

NEEDLE TEST

Through the use of self-hypnosis, the subject has anesthetized her hand. To test this anesthesia, the hypnotist pricked her palm with a hypodermic needle to observe her response. He noted the complete absence of any reflexive action. With the aid of self-hypnosis, which the subject had learned under my direction, she had been able to have dental work completed without a modicum of pain much to the amazement of her dentist.

HYPNOTISM REVEALED

THE POWERS TECHNIQUE
of
HYPNOTIZING AND SELF-HYPNOSIS
including the intriguing chapter
SLEEP AND LEARN

by **MELVIN POWERS**

Author

Self-Hypnosis
Dynamic Thinking
The Science of Hypnotism
Advanced Techniques of Hypnosis
Mental-Power Through Sleep-Suggestion

WILSHIRE BOOK COMPANY
Publishers

1324 Wilshire Blvd.
Los Angeles 17, California

Eighth Revised Edition 1956

Distributed by

Lee's Su Denity Missouri
516 W. NINTH STREET
LOS ANGELES 15, CALIF.

UNITY SCHOOL LIBRARY
Unity Village
Denity Missouri 64063

CONTENTS

COPYRIGHT 1949 BY MELVIN POWERS
Printed in the United States of America

TBF
1141
P68
1957

FOREWORD

HYPNOTISM IS ONE of the most remarkable phenomena known to man. It is as old as the human mind, as aged as the beginning of the world. To whatever quarter we direct our research, whether to dusty old manuscripts or to ancient hieroglyphics, we find indelible traces of the influence of hypnotism.

There is nothing mysterious about the phenomenon of hypnotism. However, people have long looked upon hypnosis as being surrounded by a veil of mystery. The word itself seems to carry a connotation of mysticism. It must be clearly recognized that there is nothing abnormal about it. Its principles are evident in everyday life without attracting any particular degree of attention. Suggestibility is a normal characteristic of the mind.

The successful utilization of hypnosis in the treatment of war neuroses has aroused considerable interest in hypnotism. Hypnotism received widespread recognition in World War II because it provided a means of brief and effective psychiatric treatment. Many newspapers and magazines have contained numerous articles on the use of hypnotism in the treatment of mental and physical disorders. This information has helped in bringing to the public the practical applications of hypnosis, and at the same time has dispensed with the supposed dangers that are commonly believed connected with its use.

That many permanent therapeutic cures have resulted

[13']

from the utilization of hypnosis is an indisputable fact.
Hypnotism, by relieving worry, pain and sleeplessness,
can contribute much to the comfort and cheerfulness
of the patient, thus leading to the restoration of his
health. It can overcome negative factors which are
serious obstacles to proper digestion and nutrition and
simultaneously afford greater resistance to germs, while
assisting in the repair of lesions. Since every physician,
either consciously or subconsciously uses suggestion in
his medical practice, it is necessary that it be organized
and used in a more methodical manner.

Many people have a fear of hypnotism and refuse
to expose themselves to it. Proper enlightenment on the
subject is the only means of counteracting these negative attitudes. Those who do not understand electric-
ity cannot comprehend why an electric bulb lights.
People who do not understand the psychological nature
of hypnotism cannot appreciate its curative power.

The deprecation of hypnosis as a therapeutic agent,
as expressed by poorly informed skeptics, cannot be
taken as a valid conclusion. A careful examination of
psychiatric facts and medical literature proves beyond
doubt the curative values of hypnosis. Medical science
has proven hypnotism to be a powerful tool in psychiatric therapy. Hypnotism is the key which will enable you
to reach your subconscious mind.

Melvin Powers

The History of Hypnotism

THE PRINCIPLES OF hypnotism were employed by the ancient Egyptians, and by medicine men of centuries ago, to cure diseases that had resisted normal treament. The priests of the ancient Egyptian sleep temples used the power of suggestion in curing the afflicted.

The Egyptians, Persians, Greeks and Romans were the first to recognize its force. The religious practices of certain Oriental races often used the principles of hypnotism. The laying of hands on a diseased part of the body to bring a cure dates back to the time of the Bible. In the same vein "the royal touch" of the old kings of France is reported to have effected many cures.

Anton Mesmer (1733-1815), a Viennese physician, is credited with first arousing the scientific and popular interest in hypnotism. Mesmer, long a student of astrology, believed that the planets exerted an influence on the health of human beings by magnetic attraction. He proceeded on this premise and subsequently achieved his "cures" by stroking the diseased bodies with artificial magnets.

The magnetic properties of the lodestone were well known. Its magnetic powers were believed to have an influence on the human body in combating physical ailments. The imagination of the subject plus the conscious suggestions of the operator, did actually bring about cures. Even today, amulets are worn and carried by people desiring good health, love, and wealth. The "good lucky penny" is an example of this kind of charm.

Quite accidentally, Dr. Mesmer discovered that his touch brought benefit to his patients. This shed new light on the subject of hypnotism. Through this new found knowledge, he developed the theory of Animal Magnetism, which contended that all individuals are equipped with magnetic forces which when properly controlled, could benefit and even influence other individuals. Mesmer attributed this phenomenom to an invisible fluid. This invisible agent was capable of penetrating the body, especially the nervous system. By thus influencing the organism, it brought about the desired cure.

Dr. Mesmer came to Paris under the patronage of Marie Antoinette. His clinic contained a cross-section of people from all classes and society, among them many distinguished men and women of the court of Louis XVI. To facilitate the treatment of many people, Mesmer constructed the baquet which he magnetized and which was purported to transmit the beneficial effects to the patients. It was Mesmer's practice to surround his patients with an air of mysticism. The room was dimly lighted and filled with the fragrance of sweet perfumes while strains of soft and mysterious music created atmosphere in the background.

In 1778, the French government appointed a commission composed of physicians and members of the French Academy of Science, of which Benjamin Franklin was a member, to investigate the cures. He was accused of mysticism in spite of his impressive acumulation of evidence.

One of Mesmer's disciples was the Marquis of Puysegur who revolutionized the technique of Mesmer by causing the patients to sleep through the means of hypnotic passes, thus achieving the same results as Mesmer. This method won medical approval as the hypnotic state was produced in what was considered an acceptable manner.

At this time, in England, many physicians were employing hypnosis in their treatment of disease. Dr. John Elliotson, professor of medicine at London University and president of the Royal Medical Society, was one of the leaders in this work. As one of the leading physicians and surgeons of that time, his work in the field of hypnotism aroused considerable interest in the medical profession and further advanced the science of hypnotism in the treatment of physical and mental disorders. He was one of the first to use the techniques of hypnotism in treating the mentally sick.

James Braid (1795-1860), also an English physician, was the first to discover that hypnotism was a subjective phenomenon and could be achieved without magnets and hypnotic movements of the hypnotist's hands passing over the subject's body. He discovered that by having the patient gaze at a bright object or point of concentration, the subject could be brought into a hypnotic sleep. This evidence pointed up the fact that hypnotism was attributable to physiological modifications of the nervous system and that it was also psychological since it was apparent that the subject concentrate his attention on the words of the hypnotist. It was Braid who coined the word "hypnotism" from the Greek word hypnos, meaning sleep.

Employing Dr. Braid's technique, Dr. James Esdaile of Edinburgh, (1808-1859), a surgeon in Calcutta, India, used hypnotism as an anesthetic in performing successfully more than three hundred minor and major operations, including many amputations. Today we are familiar with the use of hypnotism in dentistry and childbirth.

Dr. Lieubault (1823-1904), of France, the founder of the Nancy School of Hypnotism, and Professor Charcot (1825-1893), founder of the Salpetriere School of Hypnotism, did much to advance the medical and scientific field of hypnotism. During this period, the study of hypnotism was of tremendous importance in understanding the nature of hysteria, in which the physical symptoms, seemed similar to those that could be obtained of hypnosis. Hysteria of course refers to the development of physical symptoms without evidence of demonstrable pathology. Hysteria may be regarded as a symptom of an emotional expression which has been repressed. According to Charcot and his disciples, the hypnotic state was merely a manifestation of hysteria. They maintained its accompanying phenomena of anesthesia, catalepsy, and suggestibility could only be evoked with hysterical subjects. This view has been shown to be erroneous. All of the phenomena of hysteria can be produced with perfectly normal individuals. By using hypnotism we are able to duplicate the symptoms of various neuroses and psychoses thus making possible the investigations for their cure.

Dr. Sigmund Freud (1856-1939), studied hypnotism at the Nancy School of Hypnotism under Dr. Lieubault and Dr. Bernheim (1840-1919), as well as with Dr. Charcot. From his studies of hypnotism, Freud advanced his theories of psychoanalysis, which gave us the first modern concepts of the nature of psychogenic illness. Dr. Freud in striving to better understand the nature of mentally ill personalities, used hypnotism in his investigation of the subconscious mind. It was he who fathered the theory that cures in psychiatric therapy are achieved by revealing the causes of anxiety, rather than avoiding or skirting them. He maintained that the sooner the patient becomes better able to handle his fears and anxieties with objectivity, the quicker he will be cured. Until this time, the etiology of mental illness was practically left untouched. Freud was the first to link the etiology with the therapy. He discovered that the discharge of an emotion had a therapeutic value, and encouraged his patients to talk freely and to express deep feelings. This was the beginning of "free association" which is used so predominantly in psychoanalysis today.

Hypnotism cured battle incurred neuroses in both World Wars I and II. While under hypnosis the soldier was able to relive past experiences. The anxieties, conflicts, and fears that led to his breakdown were brought to the surface. Very often this became such a violent outpouring of deeply submerged thoughts that the doctor's questions were drowned in the torrent of words. Sometimes it was possible to remove the external symptoms of his illness in one treatment; however, it must be understood that the soldier was not fully recovered until he achieved conscious acceptance of the deep underlying disturbances which led to his breakdown. The entire field of psychotherapy has been greatly enriched by the application of hypnotism.

Facts About Hypnotism

THE FOLLOWING PARAGRAPHS contain answers to some of the most frequent questions asked about the science of hypnotism.

What is Hypnotism?

Hypnotism is a state of exaggerated or heightened suggestibility, either brought about by the hypnotist, or self-induced. Hypnotism may further be defined as a mental state resembling a sleep-like condition which is induced by psychological suggestion. Physiological reflexes, such as the patellar reflex (knee-jerk), not present in ordinary sleep, can be elicited with subjects under hypnosis. The hypnotic state is similar to the state of mind prior to sleep. It is characterized by extreme responsiveness to suggestion, acuity of intelligence and the heightened stimulation of the imagination. It is a state of extreme sensitive awareness. One in which the autonomic nervous system can be reached and easily controlled. Since the subconscious is part of the nervous system, it can be reached through hypnosis. It has been established that the mind is composed of the conscious and subconscious levels. If we look at hypnosis with these facts in mind, we can say that in the process of inducing hypnosis we put the conscious mind in a state of abeyance. This makes it possible for the subconscious mind to be reached by suggestions. In this manner, the utilization of hypnotic techniques in psychoanalysis facilitates the uprooting of the repressed underlying emotional problem, and contributes favorably to the transference between psychoanalyst and patient which is so essential to the catharsis.

Is it True That Only a Person With a Weak Will Can Be Hypnotized?

This is a popular but unjustified belief. On the contrary, the success of hypnotism depends upon a person who has a "strong will" as the individual being hypnotized must give his fullest attention to the hypnotist, while eliminating any thoughts that are not concerned with the induction of sleep. Hypnotism is a useful therapeutic tool by which the will is actually strengthened. Being able to concentrate well insures satisfactory results.

Can the Average Person be Hypnotized?

Yes. Suggestibility is a characteristic of the normal mind. We cannot hypnotize the insane, as they are living in a world of their own. Their psychological escape mechanism, turning away from reality, will not permit contact with their thoughts. The periods of attention are so short lived that hypnotizing them is impossible.

What Determines a Good Hypnotic Subject?

The subject must have the intelligence to understand what is asked of him and the ability to concentrate his thoughts upon what the hypnotist is saying. Those who can concentrate well make good hypnotic subjects. The probability of success is increased considerably when a subject can completely relax.

Is it Difficult to Awaken a Hypnotized Person?

No. There is never any difficulty in wakening a subject. You can wake him simply by saying, "Wake up." Other techniques include counting to three, clapping your hands, snapping your fingers, or using any other signal or cue, as long as a suggestion has been given previously to the subject that he will awaken when such a command is given. If the hypnotist should leave after hypnotizing a person, the subject would awaken as the rapport will have been broken. In certain cases, the subject may fall into a natural sleep and awaken later much refreshed. The problem is primarily that of putting the subject into the hypnotic state. We never encounter difficulty in waking the subject.

Will a Subject, After Awakening from the Hypnotic State, Remember What Has Occurred During the Period of Hypnosis?

In the lighter stages of hypnosis, such as the lethargic and cataleptic stages, the subject usually remembers everything that occurs. At times, in the cataleptic state, the subject may have only a partial remembrance of the events. In the deepest stage of hypnosis, the somnambulistic state, the subject has complete amnesia of the events that have taken place. If we tell him that he is to remember the details of the hypnotic state, he will recall all that has happened to him. If we suggest that he is not to remember what has occured during the hypnotic state, he will emphatically deny that he was ever under hypnosis. All efforts to prove to him that he was under hypnosis will meet with failure. Another interesting fact is that a person under hypnosis will recall all that has happened to him in previous hypnotic states if you suggest that he do so.

Can a Person Be Hypnotized Against His Will?

Under normal circumstances a person can not be hypnotized against his will by the power of suggestion. However, we can hypnotize a person by using drugs, and by so changing normal sleep into a hypnotic sleep.

Mechanical devices such as described in the following chapters will eventually break down the resistance of the subject thus allowing for quick accesss to the subconscious mind.

Are Only Gifted People Able to Hypnotize?

Anyone can learn to hypnotize. A person can get a basic understanding of hypnotism by merely witnessing the induction of hypnosis. It is erroneous to assume that only specially gifted people are able to use hypnosis. The hypnotist does not possess unusual, mysterious, or remarkable powers through which he is enabled to overcome the wills of his subjects. On the contrary, he has simply learned the techniques of inducing the hypnotic state.

Is It Possible to Induce Criminal Acts During Hypnosis?

No. A person under hypnosis will do nothing that goes against his moral code. A hypnotized subject can resist suggestions which are repugnant to him. One who is under hypnosis maintains his ego at all times and will not allow himself to deviate from his normal code of ethics. Bizarre stories dealing with hypnotism have done much injustice to the practitioners of hypnosis. The imagination of fiction writers has created many false impressions among the laity, especially concerning the influence of hypnotism on the morals of those exposed to it. This is one of the reasons that the advancement of hypnotism has been somewhat retarded.

Has Hypnotism Been Used in Surgery?

Yes. During the nineteenth century, the anesthetic properties of hypnotism were used as an aid to minor and major operations. It was also used as an anesthetic to aid in childbirth and still is used today in certain cases. Complete analgesia can be effected in any part of the body with the aid of hypnotism. With the introduction of the anesthetic properties of ether and chloroform, the use of hypnotism was gradually curtailed. It is not uncommon today to hear of cases in which dentists hypnotize their patients and then pull or drill their teeth, without the patients feeling any pain or the slightest discomfort. A newspaper article of August 25, 1946 carried the following statement of a prominent dentist, "I believe much of the unpleasantness of dentistry could be avoided by a greater use of hypnotism. After an anesthetic there is often great soreness or swelling. From my own experience with extractions under hypnotism, I have been able to successfully suggest to patients that their gums would heal quickly and cleanly. The results were excellent." In another newspaper article of April 28, 1946 a dentist claims to have filled one thousand teeth in the past year with complete absence of pain, explaining that hypnotism, rather than drugs, had done the trick. For further information relative to painless tooth extractions, observe newspaper articles in Lesson X.

In post-operative situations, where pain is persistent, hypnotism can be used to curb the pain as well as promote rapid healing. Where pain-killing anesthetics are continually used for this purpose, the patient will develop an immunity against the drug, thereafter requiring a larger dosage. The sight of the hypodermic needle to most patients has adverse psychological effects. Narcotics have a tendency to leave some patients with a feeling of nausea and sickness. This could have been avoided by using hypnotism. As for pre-operative situations, hypnotism can be especially useful in minimizing fear, anxiety, and nervousness.

Can I Hypnotize Myself?

Yes. All hypnotism is in reality a matter of self-hypnosis. The hypnotist guides the subject to sleep, but the unconscious or conscious auto-suggestions of the subject are really responsible for its attainment. The easiest way to acquire the art of self-hypnosis is to be hypnotized first, then to receive a post-hypnotic suggestion which makes it possible to go into a state of self-hypnosis at will. This establishes the basis for the conditioned reflex response. Self-hypnosis can accomplish the same therapeutic results as hetero-suggestion. Chapter V will give you detailed information on several methods of acquiring the art of self-hypnosis.

LESSON THREE

How to Hypnotize Your Subject

EVERY MENTALLY healthy person is naturally suggestible and consequently hypnotizable. Many people are extremely suggestible during the waking state. The yawning of one person will invariably cause several others to follow suit. In hypnotizing a subject when others are present, we often find that others in the group have fallen asleep.

The ability of the subject to concentrate his attention is the determining factor in the induction of hypnosis. The prime requisite is the need of gaining the attention for the purpose of directing his thoughts so that they are concentrated on one idea or along one particular channel.

We can train a person to become a good hypnotic subject. The failure to go to sleep at the first attempt does not establish him as a poor hypnotic subject. This

[28]

is also true of self-hypnosis. Hypnosis like anything else that we learn is a gradual process of development. In the training of a subject we strive for the development of a desirable conditioned reflex pattern.

Susceptibility to hypnosis increases with the repetition of the hypnotic induction of sleep, thus creating a favored pattern. The more frequently a response follows a given stimulus, the more firmly is the tendency established. This in turn becomes a conditioned response. In my private and class courses in hypnotism, I teach hypnotism and self-hypnosis on the basis of the conditioned reflex theory. A conditioned reflex response may be defined as a psychological or physiological response to a specific stimulus, resulting from training or experience.

Hypnotism may be produced by three different methods:

1. By the vocal suggestions of a hypnotist
2. By the response of the mind to one's own suggestions (self-hypnosis)
3. By the technique of fascination

With children especially, and with susceptible subjects, it is merely necessary to have them close their eyes to receive the suggestions for sleep.

People who seem to obtain results by using the Ouija board are very good subjects for hypnosis as they are susceptible to suggestion. The command to sleep is often sufficient to bring on a hypnotic sleep. The Abbot Faria, a famous hypnotist during the early part of the nineteenth century, used this technique exclusively. His procedure was to have his subjects close their eyes and after a moment had passed, he would say in a loud commanding voice: "Sleep!"

The second method concerns itself with self-hypnosis, which is a self-induced hypnotic sleep. This phase of hypnosis is fully discussed in Lesson V. The third method, which is the fascination technique, refers to the purposive tiring of the eyes as an aid in producing the hypotic sleep.

For all practical purposes it is sufficient to accept three stages of hypnosis:

1. The lethargic stage
2. The cataleptic stage
3. The somnambulistic stage

These stages refer to the depth of hypnosis, that is, the transition from a light to a deep state.

In the lethargic stage, we notice a lack of facial expression. There is perfect passivity. The eyelids are heavy or quivering. The facial muscles are completely relaxed. There may be a faint smile on the face of the subject caused by the complete relaxation of the facial muscles. The subject usually can open his eyes if challenged to do so, but often times fails to open them, saying that he prefers them closed, as opening them requires too much effort. The mind is alert and the memory is sharp. The breathing is like that of normal sleep. The subject will often comment on his pleasant and relaxed feelings.

He is alert and is able to resist suggestions.

The cataleptic stage encompasses all of the characteristics of the lethargic stage, but is a deeper stage of hypnosis. The subject cannot open his eyes. The eyeballs move upward. The eyelids do not quiver. The limbs feel very heavy. The breathing becomes slower and deeper. There is insensitivity to pain and muscular rigidity if this is suggested to the subject. It is in this state that we can inhibit motor activity. If the subject's arm or leg is placed in a certain position and suggestions given that he cannot move the limb, it will remain stationary, or in a state of rigidity until suggestions are given that the limb is to return to normalcy. The subject after awakening recalls some of the things that were said or done, but cannot remember everything.

The somnambulistic stage has all the characteristics of the cataleptic stage, but is the deepest stage of hypnosis. We find in this state that there is extraordinary immobility. The subject will not move his limbs or attempt to change his position. He will remain very passive. The subject can perform various acts that are suggested to him and is able to answer questions. However, upon awakening from the hypnotic state, we find that he has no recollection of what has occurred. He will exhibit great astonishment when told of things that he said or did and may even deny them emphatically. As in the case of amnesia or a fugue, episodes may have occurred which the person is unable to recall. There will be no recollection of what has been said or done and he may not even know that he had been hypnotized. During deep hypnosis you can give the subject suggestions to open his eyes without awakening him from the hypnotic state. He may appear to be wide awake but in reality he is still under hypnosis. In this state it is possible to produce visual hallucinations as well as auditory, gustatory and olfactory ones. There is also complete insensitivity to pain if it is suggested to him that there will be none.

In this lesson we shall deal with the fascination method principally. The other two methods are dealt with in subsequent lessons.

It is an established fact that for the induction of sleep, it is not imperative that all functions of the brain be tired. Mental or physical enervation causes sleep. If we can cause a sufficient strain on the eyes, the optic nerve would soon become tired and the muscles which hold the upper eyelid would become fatigued. We thus can induce sleep in the subject by supplementing this weariness with the proper hypnotic suggestions.

Before beginning the induction of sleep, you should clarify any misconception or fears that your subject may have in regard to the science of hypnotism. Fear and nervousness on the part of the subject can be dissipated by a frank and friendly discussion.

There are those who are afraid of hypnotism or who are reluctant to be hypnotized, but without justifiable cause. These subjects resist hypnosis consciously as well as subconsciously. Therefore it may be necessary to repeat the hypnotic procedure until their fears are eliminated. It is important to remember that susceptibility to hypnosis increases with the repetition of the hypnotic induction, thus creating a habit pattern. Tell your subject what to expect while in the state of hypnosis. This procedure is known as the "pre-hypnotic talk." The subject's confidence is gained and an air of expectancy is created which heightens the probability of inducing hypnosis.

The use of a hypnotic record, such as the one described on the back of this book, is an excellent medium of hypnotizing a subject and permits you to take complete control of the subject after hypnotism has been successfully induced. You can easily gain the subject's consent to use the hypnotic record as it is impersonal in nature and creates the atmosphere and feeling of a genuine psychological experiment. The record has a very lulling and soothing musical background and actually facilitates the successful induction of a deep state of hypnosis.

The following procedure should be used to hypnotize your subject:

Seat him in a comfortable chair or have him recline on a couch. Be sure that he is comfortable. Take some bright object or a small crystal ball and hold it about twelve inches above the subject's eyes. If you prefer, you can have him pick a spot on the ceiling and continue to have him look at it as you proceed with the induction of hypnosis. Tell him to gaze intently at the object that you are holding in your hand, or on the spot on the ceiling. Begin the hypnotic formula, speaking in a low, soothing and firm voice. Speak slowly and distinctly. Pause after each suggestion and repeat each twice, as hypnotic suggestions become better implanted in the subconscious mind by repetition. Request the subject to focus his thoughts as suggested by you. After you have become familiar with the general pattern of inducing hypnotism and the suggestions which are essential, you can improvise extemporaneously. The hypnotic formula need not be followed verbatim. In your first attempts at hypnosis, it is best to proceed in the following manner:

"Keep looking at the object that I have in my hand. (Keep looking at the spot on the ceiling.) You will notice a very pleasant feeling of heaviness coming over your entire body and head. This soothing sensation of heaviness will gradually put you into a deep, sound, pleasant, enjoyable sleep .... Relax every muscle and nerve in your body .... Breathe slowly and deeply .... Concentrate on my voice .... Every word that I utter will put you into a deeper and sounder sleep .... Relax your body .... Your legs are becoming very heavy ... Your arms are becoming very heavy .... Your eyes are becoming very watery and heavy ... They are beginning to flutter .... You can hardly keep your eyes open .... You find it very difficult to continue looking at this object .... Continue to concentrate on my voice .... Allow your mind to become very passive .... Your head and eyes feel pleasantly tired . . . . You just want to close your eyes and fall fast asleep . . . . The moment that you close your eyes you will fall into a deep, sound, hypnotic sleep; however, you will continue to listen to my voice . . .

"When I complete the count of three, it will be utterly impossible for you to keep your eyes open . . . . . . You shall close them immediately and fall into a deep, hypnotic sleep when I complete the count of three . . . .

One . . . . (Pause) . . . . Your entire body is very heavy and sleepy . . . .

Two . . . . (Speak slowly) . . . . Your head is very heavy and tired . . . Your eyelids are quivering . . . .You just want to close your eyes and fall into a deep, deep, sound, pleasant sleep . . . .

Three . . . . . (Compelling voice) . . . . Close your eyes and fall into a deep, sound, beautiful sleep . . . . Deep sleep, sound sleep, further and further away to sleep all the time . . . .

YOU ARE NOW IN A DEEP, HYPNOTIC SLEEP AND SHALL NOT AWAKEN UNTIL I TELL YOU TO WAKE UP . . . . "

We are ready at this time to try several tests with the subject to determine how deeply he is asleep. Speak to the subject as though he were wide awake. After each test, deepen the hypnotic sleep by suggestions of relaxation and as illustrated at the end of test number one.

Test No. 1. "You are so relaxed and deeply asleep that you cannot open your eyes until I tell you to do so .... The harder you try, the more difficult it will become to do .... Try to open your eyes, you will find it impossible to do so until I tell you .... They are stuck tightly together .... "(After the subject tries and finds it impossible to open his eyes, deepen the hypnotic sleep by the following suggestions): .... "You will now fall into a deeper and sounder sleep .... Deep sleep .... Sound sleep .... "

Test No. 2. "Fold your hands in front of you .... ." (After subject folds his hands give him the following suggestions): .... "Your hands are stuck tightly together and you cannot open them until I tell you to open them .... Try, but it is impossible to do so .... "(Say to him after he fails to open his hands): .... "When I snap my fingers you will be able to pull your hands apart ... "(Snap your fingers and say): .... "Now you can pull your hands apart. Pull your hands apart immediately and fall deeper asleep .... "

Test No. 3. "I am going to rotate your hands in front of you and as I revolve one hand around the other, you will fall deeper and sounder asleep . . . . (Start rotating his hands and tell him to keep up the rotation by himself) . . . . (Now tell him) : . . . . "It is impossible for you to stop rotating your hands until I tell you to do so. Try, but it is impossible for you to stop . . . . " (When you want the subject to stop, say) : . . . . "When I snap my fingers you will be able to stop rotating your hands" . . . . (Snap your fingers and say) : . . . . "Now you can stop rotating your hands . . . . Stop immediately and fall into a deeper and sounder sleep . . . . "

Test No. 4. Raise your subject's right or left arm. Hold his arm so it is fully extended. Suggest to him that his arm is becoming rigid and stiffened at the elbow so that he cannot bend it. "Your arm is becoming stiff and rigid as a bar of steel. When I complete the count of three, it will be impossible for you to lower or raise your arm. One . . . two . . . three . . . . It is now impossible for you to bend your arm until I say so." When you wish the subject to bend his arm, say: . . . . "When I complete the count of three, you will be able to bend your arm and your arm will return to normalcy . . . . One . . . two . . . three . . . Now you can bend

your arm . . . . Fall deeper asleep . . . .
deep, sound asleep."

Test No. 5.   "When I complete the count of three
your right (left) hand will become in-
sensitive to pain. You will feel numbness coming over your entire arm and
hand. This will be a very pleasant feeling and you will not be able to feel pain.
There will be complete anesthesia of your
hand . . . One . . . two . . . three . . . Your
hand is now completely anesthetized . . .
You have no feeling in your arm or
hand." (Pinch the subject. He will not
move. You may also prick the subject
with a sterilized needle. There will be
no reflex action or indication of pain.
When you wish the arm and hand to return to normalcy, say) : . . . . "When I
complete the count of three, the numbness
in your arm and hand will disappear and
your arm and hand will return to normalcy with all feeling and sensitiveness
restored . . . One . . . two . . . three . . . .
Your arm and hand have returned to
normalcy and you have all your feelings
back again."

The technique as illustrated in test number five is
at present being used by many dentists who are utilizing the anesthetic properties of hypnosis. They are able

to completely relax their patients, both adults and children, remove the fear of dental work, and completely gain the fullest cooperation. These facts are not exaggerated. They are adequately substantiated by dentists who are now employing hypnosis and further substantiated by numerous articles in dental journals. Lesson X contains several very interesting newspaper excerpts about the use of hypnotism in the field of dentistry.

Simulation of the deeper stages of hypnosis by a subject may be detected by the needle test or by the following test using ammonia:

Test No. 6. "When I complete the count of three, you will smell the fragrance of a bottle of perfume that I shall place under your nose. You will enjoy the sweet smelling and tantalizing aroma of the perfume and you will remark about the pleasant smell of the perfume . . . .One . . . two . . . three . . . " (Open the bottle of ammonia and place it under the subject's nose. You will know instantly if he has been pretending.)

Further tests such as age regression, hallucinations, recall of forgotten memories, automatic writing, analgesia in various parts of the body, the induction of dreams while under hypnosis, and catalepsy of the entire body may be easily produced by following the pattern of the given six tests. It has been found in the age regression of the hypnotized subject that an intelligence test administered while under hypnosis at the specific age levels corresponds with scoring at the chronological age. Incidentally, the subject's handwriting at various stages of age regression will correspond and change according to that level of regression. This is another excellent test for determining the depth of hypnosis.

Let us, at this time, analyze the hypnotic induction of sleep as just presented in this chapter. As the subject looks at the crystal ball in your hand, or point of concentration on the ceiling, a feeling of heaviness in the eyelids definitely will result. This is caused by fatigue which results from keeping the eyes in this strained position. The affirmation, by the hypnotist, that the eyes are becoming tired and heavy are based on physiological considerations. The subject naturally assumes that this is due solely to your suggestions. Because of this, he immediately assumes a receptive frame of mind which sets the stage for your future suggestions.

You then suggest that his eyes are becoming so heavy and tired that he wants to close them and fall into a deep, sound sleep. Even if you did not suggest this to him, he would have a natural tendency to close his eyes because of his weariness. However, your suggestions of sleep and heaviness contribute very favorably to his desire to close his eyes. For one thing, it is easier to close them than to keep them open while in this strained position. Psychologically, the association of closing the eyes with the accompanying heaviness of the eyelids and the comfortable position of the body point the way to sleep. Here, once again, you profit by this natural physiological and psychological effect by supplementing them with further suggestions of sleep, all of which are given in a low, soothing and monotonous voice. So we observe that hypnotism is produced by a limitation of sensory impressions and by a narrowing of the consciousness.

If you should fail with test No. 1, do not proceed to the subsequent test. Try the tests in order. If you successfully complete several tests and fail on the next test, do not proceed further. Deepen the hypnotic sleep by suggestion and try again.

If your subject does not respond favorably at the first attempts to hypnotize him, do not become discouraged. Try to analyze the reason for your failure. A good policy is to ask the subject what prevented him from going under hypnosis. Profit by his answer. Many times it is necessary to adapt the mode of suggestion to the idiosyncrasies of the subject. With a refractory subject, the character of the person should be evaluated and a method chosen which would seem most likely to take effect. The spasmodic twitching of the eyelids represents the first sign of the induction of hypnotism. Here a change to a firm and assertive tone of voice suggesting sleep is invaluable. The subject will often close his eyes immediately and fall into a deep, sound, hypnotic sleep. The transition from a normal state to a hypnotic state is usually gradual. At first, the subject feels a heaviness of his eyelids, then a desire to close them, followed by noticeable difficulty in keeping them open and finally they are completely closed. Practice and observation will enable you to employ the proper use of your suggestions at the right moment so that the desirable condition can be obtained. The use of a monotonous tone will help you considerably in bringing about the desired end. We know that natural sleep can be induced by monotonous songs, such as the cradle variety. Teachers, lecturers, and speakers using a monotonous pitched voice can put us to sleep in spite of our efforts to resist it. We often hear of students falling asleep in classrooms, or of individuals falling asleep while listening to the radio.

In all attempts at hypnosis, post-hypnotic suggestions are given to prepare the subject for the next induction of hypnosis. This is done whether the subject is in a light or deep state. The suggestion that he will fall into a deeper sleep next time acts as a stimulus in conditioning the subconscious mind for future inductions of hypnosis.

After a person has once been hypnotized, you can put him to sleep again immediately by giving him a post-hypnotic suggestion while he is under the hypnosis. Here is the procedure:

"Whenever I complete the count of three, you will close your eyes and fall into a deep, sound, hypnotic sleep."

The following hypnotic formula will prove itself to be very effective. Use the technique as already mentioned; that is, speak slowly, softly and distinctly. Be sure to repeat the suggestions twice. You can add to the phraseology as you notice the various reactions of the subject. For the best results seat your subject in a comfortable chair or have him lie down on a couch. Then say:

"Take three deep breaths, then breathe normally ... One, take a deep breath." (Wait until the subject has taken the deep breath and then say) "Exhale. Take another deep breath. Inhale. Exhale. And another. Inhale. Exhale . . . .

"Close your eyes now of your own accord and breathe normally. Concentrate on my voice . . . . Exclude all other thoughts from your mind . . . . Relax your arms . . . . Relax your legs . . . . Let your body go loose . . . . Relax every muscle and nerve in your entire body . . . . Imagine now that it is a beautiful summer's day. Imagine that you are floating on a cloud. It is so quiet and peaceful and there you are at ease with the world, just drifting and dreaming as you float on and on and on." (Let your voice fade here. Try to imply by your voice that the person is actually floating further away.) . . . . You are very much at ease and completely relaxed . . . . It is such a pleasant feeling . . . . It is such a soothing and pleasant feeling; a feeling as though you just want to drift far away into a deep, sound, beautiful sleep. You are so much at ease and every muscle and nerve in your entire body is completely relaxed and at ease. You feel so pleasantly tired, so completely relaxed and tired, that you just want to fall into a deep, deep sound, comfortable sleep. Every part of your body feels so heavy and tired . . . . Let yourself fall into a deep, sound and relaxing sleep. It is going to be such a nice beautiful comfortable slumber that you will want to fall faster and faster asleep . . . . And now, when I complete the count of three you will fall into a deep sound sleep . . . .

One.   Your entire body is completely relaxed . . . . Every muscle and nerve is completely relaxed and at ease . . . . Your body feels so heavy . . . .

Two.   Your head feels so heavy and sleepy . . . . It is a pleasant feeling though, but you feel so heavy and tired . . . . You keep falling further and further to sleep . . . . Your thoughts are vanishing and all you can think of now is sleep . . . . Deep sleep. Sound asleep . . . .

Three.   You are now in a deep, sound sleep and you will continue to fall into a deeper and sounder sleep. Every word that I utter will put you into a deeper and sounder sleep . . . . You keep falling into a deeper sleep all the time. All that you can hear is my voice. You hear no other sounds. . . . . You shall not awaken until I tell you to do so. Sleep. Deep sleep. Sound asleep . . . . You are now in a deep, sound hypnotic sleep. You feel very comfortable and you are completely at ease . . . . You will be able to follow my directions without awakening . . . . Deep, sound sleep."

Proceed with the tests as previously outlined.

An effective method of inducing hypnosis is with the aid of the Powers hypnodisc spiral as shown above. The spinning spiral produces a series of optical illusions, causing immediate eye strain and fatigue. The subject feels that he is being drawn into a deep, dark, revolving cone. By your suggestions of hypnotic sleep, you can place your subject in the somnambulistic state very easily. With some subjects, hypnosis will take place almost instantaneously. This technique is often employed in stage hypnotism.

During my lectures, I place the entire hypnodisc unit on the platform without having the spiral revolve. Continuing with the lecture, I note individuals in the audience gazing intently at the hypnodisc spiral. Invariably before the end of the lecture, many will have

[45]

put themselves into a deep hypnotic state. This group self-hypnosis was achieved without my mentioning anything about the hypnodisc unit. These individuals assumed that the spiral is used to induce hypnosis and their looking at it with that thought in mind produced the hypnotic state. The Powers hypnodisc spiral can be obtained for one dollar. The Powers hypnotic crystal ball can be obtained for fifty cents.

You can also place the subject under control of some other person after he is under hypnosis by giving the proper suggestions to the subject. This is known as "shifting the rapport."

The record for group-hypnosis induces hypnosis in your subject and then gives suggestions shifting the control of the subject to you. The subject will thereafter follow your suggestions. This same technique is used for self-hypnosis.

One famous New York hypnotist has recently appeared at Carnegie Hall in New York four times within one year. Using a hypnotic record at one particular demonstration he put hundreds of people in the audience to sleep as well as his subjects on the stage. Using a similar technique on several of my radio appearances over the Columbia Broadcasting System, I succeeded in hypnotizing eighty percent of the studio audiences, at the first attempt. The same results were obtained on my television shows on KFI-TV, Hollywood.

LESSON FOUR

How to Hypnotize Refractory Subjects

The problem of hypnotizing subjects who react adversely to hypnotic suggestion is one which can be handled without too much difficulty if the hypnotic procedure is patterned to the specific personality of the individual. A good pre-hypnotic talk like the one mentioned in Lesson III, is very important for use with a refractory subject. We can train these persons to become good hypnotic subjects. The repeated inductions of sleep, acting as a stimulus, increase the suggestibility of the subject following as it does, the law of conditioned response.

A reduction in the number of afferent nerve impulses reaching the brain through the central nervous system from the sensory organs can produce sleep. This is evident when we lie down in a quiet place and notice the decrease of visual, auditory, and muscular activity. The use of a metronome or the continuance of the hypnotic suggestions in a monotonous tone induces sleep as a result of the decreased activity of the cerebral cortex. The accumulation of lactic acid in the body has a similar effect; however, for hypnotic sleep this is not essential.

My students have had remarkable success in inducing hypnosis with refractory subjects, using the following technique that is based on the above assumptions:

Have the subject lie down on a couch or assume a comfortable position. Request him to close his eyes and concentrate on the playing of the hypnotic record which is described on the back of this book. This is done while he is listening to the beat of a metronome which has been set at a tempo of 120 beats per minute. The subject is instructed to imagine that every beat of the metronome is saying "sleep" and to mentally repeat this to himself. The subject is now receiving hetero-suggestions from the recording and auto-suggestions from himself. Together they will produce the somnambulistic state.

An electric metronome is best for this purpose as the tone of the audible beat can be regulated to create a pleasant and soothing effect. The closing of the eyelids itself suggests sleep. In this manner, the anticipation produces the desired result. The relaxation of the muscles, plus the reduction in the visual field immeditely decreases the afferent nerve impulses reaching the brain. We have thus narrowed the field of attention. The subject is told that every beat of the metronome will put him into a deeper and sounder sleep. He is then directed to listen to the hypnotic record. When the subject falls asleep, you can assume the rapport as the record contains suggestions facilitating this procedure. If you do not have a record, you can use the second method of

inducing sleep as outlined in Lesson III. This technique is also appropriate for self-hypnosis.

The electric metronome has a red light which flashes off and on in synchronous tempo with the auditory beat. Another effective procedure is to have the subject fix his gaze on the intermittent flashes of light while listening to the beat of the metronome. Using suggestion, you can then proceed to hypnotize the subject utilizing visual and auditory channels. This technique should be used in a dimly lighted room as the effect of the red light is thereby enhanced.

There are those who resist hypnotism consciously or subconsciously because of their fear of hypnosis. If the proper technique is used with these persons you will often find them responding immediately to your hypnotic suggestions. Let us look at the following facts:

The greater the effort to make oneself fall sleep, the less likely it is that sleep will ensue. If we consciously attempt to force sleep, we usually remain sleepless. If we attempt to control laughter or tears under certain circumstances, we usually find it impossible. At times, when we try to remember a person's name, we are unable to do so. This is known as the law of reverse effort. The greater the effort of the night watchman to remain awake, the less likely it is that he will do so. His determination to remain awake will often act conversely. This has been illustrated many times in our classroom demonstrations in dealing with refractory subjects. We have found that a rapid technique is the best method of inducing hypnosis with resistant subjects. Many subjects who claim that they cannot be hypnotized will fall immediately into a deep sleep under the proper conditions.

Barbiturates, acting as a cortical depressant, can be used to produce hypnotic sleep when all other methods have failed. The technique is not involved, and skill can be easily acquired. Chloroform and ether were the first narcotics used to produce hypnosis. Today, various derivatives and modifications of the phenobarbital family are used. Some are better suited for the lighter stages of hypnosis while others are effective for the deeper stages. Sodium amytal and sodium pentothal are the most commonly used brief-acting barbiturates, however many others can be used. The vein selected is usually the median basilic in the antecubital fossa, or a dorsal metacarpal vein in the back of the hand. The patient is asked to count slowly during the injection, about one count per second, and loudly enough so that the voice will be audible. The injection is then stopped to permit the complete effect which usually requires thirty to thirty-five seconds, at which time the patient usually ceases to count and shows evidence of relaxation, the dropping of the jaw, etc. The drugs are administered in distilled water solution by slow intravenous injection at a rate of not more than 1 c.c. a minute. Dosage varies from 3 grains to 15 grains dissolved in 10 to 20 c.c. of distilled water. These barbiturates may also be taken in capsule form. A capsule of 1½ to 3 grains taken orally will produce a drousy state in about twenty minutes. This is supplemented by hypnotic suggestion. Even in the use of barbiturates, an understanding of the techniques and principles of hypnotism is essential to obtain the maximum benefits resulting from its utilization. During the administration of the drug the psychologist gains the patient's attention and establishes hypnotic rapport.

In psychiatric work, barbiturates are used to overcome the psychic tension of the patient which may have its roots in fear, shame, or the unconscious. While the subject is in the hypnoidal state, we find him speaking freely and divulging his conflicts, anxieties, and repressed memories. Physiologically, the barbiturates act as a depressant of the higher nerve centers in the cortex while psychologically they lessen the activity of the inhibitory centers, thus facilitating a release of inhibitions and simultaneously removing the psychic barriers.

LESSON FIVE

Self-Hypnosis
How To Hypnotize Yourself

SELF-HYPNOSIS or auto-hypnosis, has been practiced for centuries by the devotees of various religious cults. Indian ascetics who had practiced yoga and the medicine men of savage tribes who were able to anesthetize various parts of their body at will, which made it possible for them to dance barefooted on a bed of live coals, walk on broken glass, or sleep on a bed of nails, achieved those feats through self-hypnosis. They were also able to inflict severe wounds on themselves which they did not feel. In jungle tribes, the monotonous and rhythmic beating of drums struck in the same cadence, plus the expectancy of the unknown, produced various forms of psychological conditions which were analogous to hypnotic states. Here in America, there are religious groups whose principles are specifically based on the theory of auto-suggestion. These groups are increasing in large numbers.

It is self-hypnosis that explains the ability of Hindu priests and Moslem dervishes to endure excruciating pain. Their state of meditation is actually a state of self-hypnosis. The ability of certain people to wake up at an exact time is a matter of training. This is self-hypnosis, whether it is done on a conscious or subconscious plane.

In reviewing present and past hypnotic literature, we find that psychologists are in accord that all normal, healthy people can be hypnotized. It is the time element that is the varying factor in this procedure. Let it be noted that anyone can learn to hypnotize himself.

Self-hypnosis refers to a highly suggestible state of mind which a person produces consciously or subconsciously. The proper utilization of self-hypnosis can be instrumental in overcoming many mental and physical disorders. Thoughts are mental impulses which have definite effects either good or bad on the body or mind. We can see this readily in cases of physical disorders, such as gastric ulcers and gastroduodenal disorders, and also in mental disorders such as psychasthenia, hypochondria, and hysteria. These conditions are usually precipitated by worry, nervous tension, or emotional disturbances. An individual suffering from slight indigestion may believe himself to have heart disease and will promptly suffer palpitations and breathlessness. After a medical examination and a reassurance that he has no heart disease, his symptoms may vanish. A common heart symptom, angina pectoris, is often found to be psychological in origin. By using self-hypnosis, proper suggestions can be given to intensify the desirable mental impulses for the purpose of eliminating various mental and physical disorders. If the rays of the sun fall on your hand, you will feel its warmth. If you place a lens over your hand, it will produce a blister or a burn. Self-hypnosis acts just like that lens. A similar kind of channel has been created through which thoughts pass, as the sun rays had passed through the lens. If the mind is powerfully stimulated it will react upon the body. A man may be fatigued, too tired to move, even too drowsy to concentrate. Suddenly, someone says to him, "Your child's life is in danger, you can save her." The mind is immediately galvanized into action. The body as a result loses its sense of fatigue and is energized. It is the same way that self-hypnosis can work for you. It is an achievement of self-control and self-direction through a heightened consciousness of purpose. The entire field of psychosomatic medicine is based on the inter-relationship of mind and body. Anxieties may manifest themselves through feelings of physical discomfort.

To fully understand self-hypnosis, we must have a clear picture of the nature of conditioned reflexes. A conditioned reflex may be defined as a psychological or physiological response to a specific stimulus resulting from training or experience. It is established by the repetition by a given stimulus or procedure. These responses then become involuntary.

The first stages of swallowing food are a voluntary action; however, once the food reaches the pharynx, an involuntary reflex control is established. When we take food into the mouth, an increased flow of saliva results. This action is an unconscious reflex response. The smell, thought or sight of food can also bring on a similar response. A conditioned salivary response may be elicited when we hear the tone of the dinner gong or smell the aroma of food in the kitchen.

SELF-HYPNOSIS

I. P. Pavlov, the well-known psychologist, experimented with dogs to study the nature of these conditioned responses. He found that if a bell is rung at the same time that food is given to a dog and that if this is continued for an interval, the dog will salivate in response to the bell, even though no food is offered. An unconscious physiological reflex has thus been established.

A friend of mine, who owns several pastry shops, increased his business considerably by following my suggestion utilizing the involuntary reflex pattern. I suggested that he keep the doors of his pastry shops open to allow the aroma of the delicacies to permeate the outside air. People walking by the pastry shops sensed the pastry. This caused a stimulation of sensory cells in the olfactory membranes of the nasal cavity. These in turn sent afferent nerve impulses to the salivary center of the brain. Efferent nerve impulses were then relayed to the salivary glands which stimulated the salivary glands to secrete saliva. This in turn produced a desire for the pastry. The result—increased sales.

The training of a dancing bear is accomplished by having the bear walk over warm coals on his hind legs while a fiddler renders a lively tune. The instinct of the bear is to raise his foot high in the air every time his foot touches the coal to avoid the discomfort of the heat. After this procedure is carried out for a certain duration, the bear will lift his hind legs (dance) whenever the fiddler plays the tune even though the bear is not walking on warm coals. An involuntary conditioned reflex has been established. Here the memory of

the painfulness of the experience plus the stimulus of the music instills an involuntary reflex pattern. Horses and dogs are also trained by this method.

A person need only be frightened once by a dog to develop permanent fear of all dogs. Similarly, a person need have only one terrifying experience in learning to swim to make him fearful of ever learning to swim again. The association of fear with dentists actually keeps many people away from seeing a dentist even though they are in need of treatment. The finger manipulation necessary to the playing of the violin and other musical instruments as well as the use of the typewriter become automatic after the conditioning process has been established.

The contraction of the pupil of the eye caused by light is an example of an automatic involuntary response. By hypnosis, we can cause the pupil to remain constant, thus inhibiting the optic nerve, or we can cause the pupil to contract by suggestion. The contraction of the pupil is an automatic pupillary reflex. The blinking of the eyelids may be classified in the same reflex category.

Many functions of the body are involuntary; however, they are not entirely separated from consciousness. We see this in the respiratory, digestive, and circulatory systems, also in the secretory functions of the glands. All these functions are regulated by the autonomic (involuntary) nervous system. The autonomic nervous system is primarily reflexive in action and is influenced through the central nervous system

by the channels of suggestion and emotion. Organs like the heart and kidneys are also involuntary in regulation; however both are easily affected by emotional experiences.

In one of our classes, a student was suddenly taken with a fit of sneezing when another student and his wife walked into the lecture room after the lecture had already started. After violently sneezing for a minute he asked the student's wife if she would remove the roses from her hat and leave it with the receptionist as he was allergic to roses. Upon being informed that they were artificial roses, the sneezing stopped immediately. Once again, we see the involuntary reflex pattern. We know that many allergies are psychological in origin. Asthma attacks are frequently associated with emotional conflicts.

The goal in learning self-hypnosis is to establish a conditioned reflex to a specific stimulus as illustrated in the previous cases. This is done by repeatedly practicing or experiencing definite stimuli that produce hypnosis. At the school, we teach self-hypnosis, to the playing of the record for self-hypnosis as described on the back of this book. We instill a conditioned reflex pattern to the hypnotic induction of self-hypnosis. This conditioning is augmented by the post-hypnotic suggestion that the subject will be able to induce self-hypnosis by using the hypnotic formula which is given in the record. Thus, we see the conditioning plus the post-hypnotic suggestions of self-hypnosis working in the subject's favor. After this has been established, the

original stimulus is replaced by a hypnotic formula which takes only five seconds to complete the hypnosis. The learning pattern is similar to that used in the conditioning of the dogs to the sound of the bell.

Think of your favorite food. Doesn't your mouth water immediately? That is just how long it takes to produce self-hypnosis once the involuntary reflex has been established.

Reflex patterns may be achieved consciously. A mother is usually not disturbed by the loud snoring of her husband, but the moment her baby makes the slightest noise, she immediately awakens. A physician in one of our classes, whose sleep was disturbed by street noises at night, trained himself to wake up only in response to the sound of the telephone.

We can also set up a conditioned reflex pattern for self-hypnosis by practicing the following hypnotic formula.

The suggestions may be given to yourself either silently or aloud. Seat yourself in a comfortable chair or recline on a couch. Choose a spot on the ceiling and continue to look at it. Then give yourself these hypnotic suggestions. Repeat the suggestions several times.

> "Presently I shall notice a very pleasant feeling of heaviness coming over my entire body . . . . Every muscle and nerve in my entire body is completely relaxed and at ease . . . . My legs are getting very heavy . . . . My arms are getting very heavy . . . . My entire body is very heavy and sleepy . . . . . My head and eyes feel

very tired now, and I just want to close my eyes and fall fast asleep . . . . My eyes are becoming very watery . . . . My eyelids are becoming very heavy, and I just want to close my eyes and fall fast asleep . . . . The moment that I close my eyes I shall be in a deep, sound, hypnotic sleep . . . . I shall be able to give myself suggestions and I shall be able to wake up at will . . . . When I complete the count of three, it will be utterly impossible for me to keep my eyes open and I shall close them and fall into a deep sound sleep . . . . One, two, three . . . . deep sleep, sound sleep, fast sleep . . . . I am now in a deep hypnotic sleep and I can give myself post-hypnotic suggestions. I have perfect control of myself, and can wake up at will . . . . Deep sleep . . . . Sound asleep . . . ."

Another excellent technique for achieving self-hypnosis as well as hetero-hypnosis is with the use of the hypnodisc spiral as shown on page 45. The spiral is attached to a phonograph motor and as it revolves, you concentrate on its center. You will note various optical illusions and the pleasant, relaxed feeling that accompanies these illusions. Giving yourself suggestions of hypnotic sleep, you find that you are easily able to attain the desired state of self-hypnosis. This is a very successful method of inducing self-hypnosis. The hypnodisc spiral is printed on firm cardboard. It measures twelve inches in diameter and has a hole in its center so you can place it on your own phonograph turntable. It has the general appearance of a twelve inch phonograph record. The Powers hypnodisc spiral can be obtained for one dollar by writing to me. The spiral can be used when it is stationary. Concentrate on the spiral shown on page 45 and you will get its hypnotic effect immediately.

In reality, all hypnotism is a matter of self-hypnosis. The hypnotist guides the subject into the hypnotic state by proper suggestions of sleep. The subject, by his own auto-suggestion, enters the hypnotic state. Thus, we can see that every person who has been hypnotized is capable of learning self-hypnosis very readily.

The purpose in teaching the patient self-hypnosis is to prove to him that he can benefit by suggestions brought about by his own desire. In this manner, he is able to control anxiety or depressed feelings. Subsequently, he learns that he is able to cope with his problem without depending solely on the hypnotist for the therapeutic cure.

In giving yourself therapeutic suggestions by using self-hypnosis, it is not necessary to be in a deep state of hypnosis as is commonly believed. A lighter stage is preferable as it is easier on his level to have a clear active and alert mind when giving suggestions. It is not the purpose of hypnosis to have the subject act as an automaton. On the contrary, we develop a state in which the body is completely relaxed, allowing for close contact with the autonomic nervous system.

In utilizing self-hypnosis, a person's powers of concentration could be augmented by the elimination of undesirable sounds through the technique of negative auditory hallucination. If suggestions are given to a hypnotized subject that he will hear no sound except the voice of the hypnotist, the subject will be oblivious to all other voices or sounds. A sudden loud noise or even the shooting of a gun will not disturb him. This has been experimentally proven many times. If self-hypnosis had been taught to men in the armed forces, they could have slept through the worst bombardments. If wounded, they would have been able to anesthetize the wounded area and eliminate pain.

The following is an original idea that I have successfully developed over a period of many years in training individuals for self-hypnosis. Self-hypnosis can be achieved with the aid of the sleep-o-matic tape recorder. These units contain a clock with quarter-hour controls that can be pre-set to start and stop the recording tape automatically. An under-the-pillow speaker is used to transmit the sound solely to the sleeper. The subject, before going to sleep at his regular time, sets the tape recorder to play at various intervals during the night. The suggestions of hypnosis which have been previously recorded are then impressed in his subconscious mind during sleep and self-hypnosis can thus be attained.

For those of you who are especially interested in learning more about self-hypnosis, I have written a book devoted to this fascinating subject. This book is described on page 114. I would highly recommend it to you.

The following article from the May 28, 1951 issue of Newsweek will give you further information as to the practicality of this technique.

BRAVE NEW RECORDINGS

"I can rid myself of any symptoms, completely and in less than a minute," drones the loudspeaker. "I'm not overly dependent on medicine or on doctors," the confident voice continues. Then in a monotone, over and over: "My mind is a blank. I am relaxing . . . relaxing . . ."

By amplified tape recording, recitations of this kind in otherwise quiet hospital wards are now relieving the "terror dreams" of mentally ill war veterans. Within three to four weeks of the "suggestion" treatment, which follows the simple principles of hypnosis (and some imaginative scenes from Aldous Huxley's "Brave New World"), most patients report gratifying results. Dr. Ernst Schmidhofer of Kennedy Veterans Hospital, Memphis, Tenn., told his colleagues at the American Psychiatric Association meeting in Cincinnati, of the success of this new technique which is being applied at his institution.

Some of the men are able for the first time in their lives to nap in the daytime. Sleep is more quiet and refreshing. Patients dream less or have pleasant dreams instead of nightmares. Almost no one except newly admitted men ask for sleeping pills. Dr. Schmidhofer added that there is "much less arising to smoke and to pace about restlessly."

Patients at Kennedy Veterans Hospital get the "sleep program" every night from 10 p.m. to 7 a.m. There is a much shorter daytime treatment. The loudspeakers are in the ward and the recorder in the nurse's office. Dr. Schmidhofer recommends the use of this method to bring much-needed restful sleep and relaxation to patients suffering from all types of mental illness, psychosomatic ailments, and pains of various sorts.

How to Awaken
Your Subject or Yourself from Hypnosis

DO NOT WORRY about waking up a subject as this is not a problem. It is however necessary to know how to awaken the subject properly. The following question is often asked:

"What would happen to the hypnotized subject in case of a sudden emergency?"

Under hypnosis, the subject has complete control over his mental and physical self at all times. A mother can sleep through the worst thunderstorm, but the moment her baby cries in his room, she immediately wakes up. The subconscious mind never sleeps.

Some subjects will awaken when the hypnotist stops talking to them. The fact that he has stopped talking acts as a suggestion to awaken. Others may be awakened by an unexpected or loud noise. As a general rule, you will never encounter any difficulty in waking your subject.

You can awaken a subject by merely saying, "Open your eyes and wake up." For self-hypnosis, "I shall open my eyes and wake up." Remember, you must give him the suggestion to open his eyes, as you told him previously that he will not be able to do so until you tell him to open his eyes.

The following method of awakening the subject gives healthful suggestions at the same time:

"When I complete the count of three, you will open your eyes and wake up feeling fine . . . . You will awaken feeling full of vim, vigor, and vitality . . . . You will be wide awake and feel perfectly well . . . . One, two, three . . . . open your eyes and feel fine."

An excellent technique is to suggest to the subject that he count aloud to ten to awaken. At the count of five, suggest that he will open his eyes and when he completes the count of ten he will be completely wide awake. If your subject awakens from a deep state of hypnosis, he will be unable to explain why he was counting. The suggestions are as follows:

"When I complete the count of three, you will begin to count aloud to the count of ten . . . . When you reach the count of five you will open your eyes, and when you complete the count of ten you will be completely wide awake . . . . One, two, three. Begin counting . . . ."

For self-hypnosis:

"When I complete the count of three, I shall open my eyes and wake up feeling fine . . . . I shall awaken feeling full of vim, vigor, and vitality . . . . I shall be wide awake and feel perfectly well . . . . One, two, three . . . . I shall now open my eyes and feel fine."

The Psychology of Hypnotism
Post-Hypnotic Suggestion

A POST-HYPNOTIC suggestion is a suggestion that is given to the hypnotized subject which is to be executed by him after he has been awakened.

I gave a hypnotized subject, an ardent cigarette smoker, the suggestion that after he woke up, every cigarette that he smoked would taste stale to him, and that he would throw the cigarette away after the second puff. After I awakened him, we continued with the general conversation. I casually lit a cigarette and the subject followed suit. After he took the first puff, he remarked that the cigarette had a "funny taste." I ignored his remark and continued with the conversation. With his second puff he made a grimace like one taking castor oil, and threw away his cigarette in disgust. I, of course, was very sympathetic with him and offered him one of my cigarettes. The same thing took place. He concluded that the weather had made the cigarettes taste badly. Even though I pointed out to him that I was smoking the same brand of cigarettes, he persisted in his conviction. I then pointed out to him that he was acting in accordance with a post-hypnotic suggestion that I had given him while he was under hypnosis. He had no recollection of my implanting this suggestion in his subconscious mind, and was not convinced of the fact until I re-hypnotized him and removed the suggestion.

To understand fully what happens in the execution of hypnotic suggestions, we must realize that the mind is composed of the conscious and subconscious levels. The existence of this fact is demonstrated by the preceding cigarette smoking situation. Certain phenomena of everyday life give us an indication of the working of the subconscious mind. We may suddenly remember a name which our conscious mind had previously attempted to recall. I am sure that you have occasionally heard a person, who was trying to remember something, say, "If I stop thinking about it, it will come to me." When an individual is confronted with a decision, he may remark, "Let me sleep on it" or "Let me sleep on the problem." Oftentimes upon awaking from his sleep he finds that he has arrived at a solution of his problem. Another example is the case of the sleep-walker, medically known as a somnambulist. Webster's New International Dictionary defines a somnambulist as: One who is subject to somnambulism; one who walks in his sleep; a sleep-walker. Somnambulism is defined as: A sleep or sleeplike state in which walking or others acts are performed. These acts are, typically, not remembered in the subsequent waking state, but may be recalled in a later attack.

Many people talk in their sleep. We can often carry on an intelligent conversation with persons in this state of mind. Yet, upon awakening, they have no knowledge of what has been said or will even go as far as to deny the fact that they had spoken to us. Upon awakening, a subject may not recall any of the details of the hypnotic state; however, upon being hypnotized again he will remember all that happened during the previous hypnosis if this is suggested to him.

A sleep-walker (somnambulist) may get up at night, dress himself, walk about the house, perform certain acts or accomplish certain work and return to bed. He will be amazed himself, the next day, to find work completed which he had apparently left uncompleted. This is a familiar illustration of a psychological state of mind in which consciousness has been suspended, whereby his actions were accomplished without his being consciously aware of it. What force has his body obeyed? What is the contributing factor that made possible the execution of these acts of dressing, walking and working? The answer lies in the unconscious or subconscious mind.

If we can understand the nature of hypnosis and post-hypnotic suggestion in terms of the subconscious mind then we can better understand the nature of fugues and amnesia cases in which there are prolonged psychological conditions characterized by wandering and unusual actions of which, later, the individual is not conscious.

[67]

During Dr. Anton Mesmer's time, the phenomenon of hypnotism was looked on as being due to the "power" of the hypnotist. Dr. James Braid's theory was that hypnotism was a subjective phenomenon. In other words, the subject put himself under hypnosis. Charcot, contended that hypnosis could only be produced in hysterics, believed further that hypnotism was due to somatic changes in the hypnotized individual. Here hypnotism was also looked upon as a matter of dissociation, caused by neurophysiological changes in the cortex. It might be mentioned that Charcot's work dealt almost entirely with hysterics. Lieubault and Bernheim, who opposed him in this view, were general practitioners, and had used hypnotism to cure just about everything conceivable in the medical dictionary. They contended that hypnotism could be induced in all individuals. One of Bernheim's theories was that there was no such thing as hypnotism. It was all a matter of suggestion. Emile Coue, a French pharmacist, founded the school of auto-suggestion based upon this premise. The psychoanalytical theory is that the subject's desire to attain the hypnotic state sets a goal for him whereby he attempts to conform to the behavior pattern of the hypnotized. Freud's premise was that it fulfilled a need for submission. He further stated that libidinal drives were also somewhat gratified in the nature of hypnosis.

All these theories are valid to some degree, under particular conditions in certain cases. They are naturally based upon the psychologist's particular school of thought or psychodynamic approach to psychology. Even the use of the electroencephalograph indicating various brain waves has shown conflicting results. The problem is still unsettled and certainly a great deal of intensive and extensive work must be done in this direction.

What are your views on the theory of hypnosis? Can you discern the correlation between the various abnormal psychological phenomena and various characteristics of hypnotism?

Hypnotism today is the key that unlocks the door to amnesia. Hypnotism has been used repeatedly with great success in the treatment of amnesia victims. A person suffering from this condition is hypnotized and while in this state the hypnotist probes the subconscious mind and exposes the events as well as the causative factors that lead to his condition.

The patient who is desirous of hypnotic therapy is actually on the road to recovery before he begins his treatment. He has been assured or has convinced himself that hypnosis can cure him of his particular problem. This conviction lends itself to reassuring suggestions that bring in its train positive thoughts for recovery.

Subjects who simulate the characteristics of a hypnotized person often will fall into a deep hypnotic sleep.

Post-hypnotic suggestions will often work with these subjects and they will find it impossible to resist them.

I shall cite an example of this phenomenon. In one of our hypnotism classes, a guest of one of the students asked to be hypnotized. I proceded to hypnotize him by the "fascination method," a procedure that involved his looking into my eyes. Within a minute he was apparently in a hypnotic sleep. I tried several tests with him and he executed them too well; that is, he did not show the customary characteristics. We knew that he was pretending, but I continued to work with him deepening the supposed hypnotic sleep. After having him perform several simple tasks, I gave him a post-hypnotic suggestion to scratch his head every time I touched my chin and then woke him up. I continued with the lecture and about five minutes later touched my chin. The subject immediately started to scratch his head. This was repeated many times within the next two hours with the same results. The subject related to the class that he did not feel that he was hypnotized, but was still unable to resist the impulse to scratch his head at the given signal. So you see, a subject need not be in a deep stage of hypnosis to carry out post-hypnotic suggestions.

When hypnotism was in its infancy in the days of Mesmer, the induction of hypnotism took between thirty minutes to one hour. Today, with our extensive knowledge of this science, hypnotism can be induced quicker than you can recite the nursery rhyme "Jack and Jill."

As soon as the proper mental attitude has been formulated in the subject's mind you can induce hypnotism within five seconds by merely saying, "Sleep." The stage hypnotist invariably uses this rapid technique which takes only several seconds to induce complete hypnosis. With susceptible subjects, it is only necessary to give them the cue as to when to fall asleep.

> "When I complete the count of three, you will close your eyes and fall into a deep sound sleep . . . . One, two, three, close your eyes and sleep."

It is a scientific fact that once a person has been hypnotized, the hypnotist can put the person to sleep again by merely snapping his fingers, counting to three, clapping his hands or by any other given signal provided the proper suggestions have been given during the last hypnosis. This is accomplished by the medium of a posthypnotic suggestion. This method is also the easiest way to teach a person self-hypnosis. You give the hypnotized subject the suggestion that he will fall asleep immediately whenever he mentally completes the count of three or snaps his fingers. The subject is thus trained to hypnotize himself at will within a matter of seconds.

The following technique is used to hypnotize a subject at a future time. While the subject is under hypnosis, the hypnotist suggests that when he wakes up, he will fall asleep immediately whenever he (the hypnotist) snaps his fingers or gives some other signal. The suggestion is:

"Whenever I snap my fingers you will close your eyes and fall into a deep, sound sleep immediately."

The subject will from that time on fall asleep immediately whenever you snap your fingers, count to three, or by any other given signal provided the suggestions have been given to him. This is one of the remarkable phenomena of hypnotism. In fact, this is often done in psychotherapeutic work in order to save time, avoiding the longer techniques of re-hypnotizing the subject for each visit. The patient is conditioned for this by previous post-hypnotic suggestions. Here again is evidence of the training of a conditioned response pattern to a specific stimulus.

Post-hypnotic suggestions may be effective for months and even years after the original post-hypnotic suggestion was given. A physician, from Chicago, who had taken my course in hypnotism came to Hollywood on a business matter and visited one of our classes. In demonstrating the phenomenon of post-hypnotic suggestion with one of the students, I used a certain key phrase for the induction of hypnosis. I was surprised to see that the physician had fallen asleep instantaneously. Upon further investigation, we discovered that that I had previously conditioned him to fall asleep with this same phrase. I hadn't seen the doctor for more than a year; however, the post-hypnotic suggestion had been effective immediately.

Psychotherapy

HYPNOTISM IS A valuable aid in the treatment of cases that have not proved amenable to ordinary medication. I feel that it is destined to play an important role in the treatment of diseases and in the alleviation of human suffering.

We have in hypnosis a powerful curative agent for certain types of diseases. If judiciously applied, it is capable of doing great good in the amelioration of these diseases. It may also act as a palliative. Hypnotism not only affords a cure for certain mental disorders, but offers aid for many physical disorders of a functional character. Many seemingly organic ailments are physical manifestations of a neurosis. These physical disturbances are eliminated when the mental conflict is resolved. Every physician either consciously or subconsciously uses suggestion in his medical practice. Why shouldn't it be used in a more organized and methodical manner so its effectiveness may be further extended? The trained nurse knows the importance of psychological factors in medicine and fully realizes that the mind as well as the body must be treated. This is done through the establishment of confidence and the promotion of a cheerful atmosphere. The expectant recovery is also discussed with confident anticipation.

Hypnotism has been used very successfully in overcoming various problems such as alcoholism, excessive smoking, stuttering, insomnia, inferiority complexes, and nailbiting. Various menstrual irregularities are often curable through hypnotic suggestion. Dietary control can be improved to a point where it is possible for a person to diet without unfavorable effects. The temptation to eat sweets or certain foods can be adequately controlled by posthypnotic suggestions.

Many phobias, such as claustrophobia (fear of inclosed places), agorophobia (fear of open places), hydrophobia (fear of water), and zoophobia (fear of animals) can be eliminated by hypnoanalysis. Compulsions commonly termed manias, such as kleptomania (compulsion to steal), pyromania (compulsion to destroy by fire), and dipsomania (compulsion for indulgence in alcohol) can also be overcome through hypnosis. It is necessary to fully comprehend the causes of the fear or compulsion. Its dynamic significance must then be made clear to the patient.

Complete sexual and mental compatibility is the goal

of every marriage. A successful marriage necessitates the fullfillment of both of these factors before complete happiness can be achieved. Too often we find that sexual disturbances, such as frigidity in women and impotence in men, are the leading causative factors in an unhappy marriage. Nagging, irritability, and infidelity may have their origin in unsatisfactory sexual release. A harmonious marriage cannot be attained unless normal mutual needs are satisfied. Abnormalities are always interrelated with the patient's total personality. The treatment necessarily involves the entire personality structure and not merely the symptom. Through hypno-analysis, the conflicts and drives which are the basis of these sexual abnormalities are uncovered. The patient, aided by insight learns the significance of the repressed factors and prepares to solve his problem with the proper direction.

Psychoanalysis is based upon the principle that neurotic illness is the result of unpleasant experiences or thoughts that have been forced into the subconscious mind. These repressions later return in a disguised form of a mental or physical disorder. Freud found that the repression was usually of an instinctive emotion. A cure results only when the unconscious conflict is brought to the level of consciousness and faced squarely by the patient. In psychoanalysis, free association and dream analysis are the two main techniques used in uprooting the repressions. This procedure usually involves a long period of time. The fields of hypno-analysis and narco-analysis which utilize hypnotism as an effective and rapid aid in probing the subconscious mind, have been very helpful in obtaining cures. The purpose of analysis is not necessarily to learn the facts but to release emotion.

In the treatment of any nervous functional disorder or any other disorder where it is desirous to employ hypnotism, it is imperative to remember that the symptom is primarily an indicator of the maladjustment of the personality. It may be likened to a clock which has stopped running. We know that there is something internally wrong when this happens. The causes of these personal disturbances often have their origin in childhood and may be completely forgotten, even though they may still continue to motivate behaviour. Deepseated conflicts having their roots in early childhood are more difficult to eradicate than those acquired in later years. Incidents that have been forgotten or repressed by the conscious mind can be brought to the surface through specialized techniques of hypnosis. We are able thus to uncover neurotic defense mechanisms in a comparatively short time. It is essential that not only the psychological disturbance be studied, but also that the personality structure and environment of the individual be taken into consideration for the most effective treatment.

In all cases, it is necessary to remove the cause of anxiety and to give the patient an insight into the unconscious mechanisms which are responsible for his symptoms. This must be done before a real cure is insured. The sooner the patient faces his anxiety and fear with objectivity, the quicker he will be aided. Hypnotism is the tool of psychiatry that makes it possible to reach the subconscious mind.

The Rorschach test is another means of securing information about the personality structure which can not always be determined by interviews. The Rorschach test, constructed by the Swiss psychiatrist, Hermann Rorschach, consists of a series of ten ink blots. On each card there is a symmetrical ink blot form which is ambiguous as to its meaning, but which suggests certain pictures or ideas to the subject. These forms are sometimes referred to as "ink blots." As the subject is shown each card, he is asked, "What does this suggest to you?" The test is scored on the basis of each response and the frequency with which certain responses occur.

The Thematic Apperception Test will also help us to uncover subconscious material. Here, the patient is shown a series of pictures, one at a time, each representing an independent scene. He is asked to discuss the relationship of the individuals in the picture, to suggest what has happened to them, and to describe their present feelings and thoughts. The future of the card characters are also considered. This is all embodied in a story. The purpose of the test is hidden from the patient as he is told that this test is a measure of his creative imagination. An analysis of the various stories will reveal predominant trends in the patient's character structure.

The analysis of dreams also enables us to further our study of the patient's subconscious motivations. In dreams, conscious as well as repressed desires, appear in symbolic form. Often by the proper interpretation of these symbolic forms we are able to secure information which otherwise could never have been elicited by clinical interviews.

Hypnotism is not a panacea to end all neurotic ills; however, it definitely has a leading role in the field of psychotherapy. The entire fields of hypno-analysis and narco-synthesis are dependent upon the utilization of the hypnotic techniques before psychoanalytical procedures can be used. Hypno-analysis is the science by which psychoanalytical treatment is abbreviated by the employment of hypnosis. The field of narco-synthesis employs the use of a barbiturate in order to lessen the ego resistance to treatment. Psychoanalytical principles are then applied. Even in the use of a narcotic, hypnotic techniques are utilized in conjunction with the administration of the drug.

Psychotherapy is often dependent upon suggestive therapy. Hypnotism is employed to fit the particular case involved. The verbal assurance of the doctor that a condition will be alleviated by taking "the bitter medicine" is often sufficient to bring about the cure.

If the patient's mental attitude towards hypnosis is that of incredulity and prejudice, the probability of successful results are minimized. Suggestion is most effective with a receptive mind. The patient should be convinced that benefits are to be derived. The manner in which the suggestions are given must be suited to the individual patient. This is an important point to remember. Some will respond better to a soothing manner whereas others are more receptive to an authoritative voice. The ensuing suggestions will serve as a guide in achieving effective psychological results. To help yourself, give yourself the same suggestions using the pronoun (I) instead of (YOU).

ALCOHOLISM

In treating the alcoholic, it is necessary to know that alcoholism is a symptom of a maladjusted personality. The alcoholic is an individual who is escaping from intolerable stress or conflicts. He is unable to adjust to life situations in a normal fashion and escapes temporarily by achieving the false self-assurance that alcohol brings. Total abstinence is an essential prerequisite for his cure. He must be taught how to meet his daily problems in an adult and realistic manner. As is true of a majority of mental patients, his emotional life has not developed to a point of maturity. If it has, he has not been able to sustain himself on that level for long. For permanent recovery, the patient must understand the primary causes of his emotional distress which lie hidden in the deep recesses of his mind. In order to cure him it is necessary to stress the following four suggestions. He is told he dislikes liquor, the taste is repugnant and nauseating, he doesn't crave liquor at all, and that he has strengthened his self-control. I would also seek the help of the Alcoholics Anonymous group in your community. If there is no local group listed in your phone book, write to: The Alcoholic Foundation, Box 459, Grand Central Annex, New York 17, N. Y. You will receive the address of your nearest group, and confidential advice in dealing with the problem.

The suggestions should be worded in the following manner:

> "From this moment forth, you (I) will have an intense dislike for alcoholic beverages . . . . Alcoholic drinks will have a repugnant and nauseating taste . . . . You (I) no longer will have a craving for alcoholic drinks and will be perfectly content to do without them . . . . Moreover, your (my) self-control will be greatly increased and you (I) shall be able to withstand the temptations of drinking."

STUTTERING

Stuttering may be caused by a traumatic experience, imitation, injury or illness. Whatever the cause may be, the results are basically the same — a psychic block resulting in a lack of proper coordination between the brain and vocal organs.

If the stutterer can do any of the following with perfect speech, he has an excellent chance of recovery because his problem is psychological rather than organic.

1. Sing.
2. Speak in unison.
3. Whisper.

4. Speak when alone.
5. Speak to animals.

Some people believe that nervousness is the cause of stuttering. On the contrary, nervousness may be the result of the speech impediment. Very often as soon as the stuttering ceases, the nervousness disappears. Is the stutterer nervous when he has perfect control of speech under certain conditions such as singing or speaking in unison?

It is especially important that the stutterer is not scolded or ridiculed because of his impediment. You must realize that the stutterer needs greater love and understanding than those who do not stutter. A happy and healthy mind is naturally an adjunct to therapy. The stuttering problem in most cases starts in early childhood as there is rarely ever a case of stuttering that develops after a person has reached his twelfth birthday.

The general methods used today by speech schools and speech therapists are to teach the stutterer diaphragmatic breathing, articulation, phonetics, voice and speech exercises. They teach the stutterer to overcome the "hard words," for instance the ones beginning with 'd' and 'n.' They also teach the stutterer to speak in a sing-song fashion. The deeper causes of defective speech are sometimes left untouched. This results in a continuance of the defective speech pattern. Most therapists put a great deal of emphasis on the importance of proper breathing for the cure of stammering. They fail to realize that faulty breathing is often attributable to the tensions developed in the abdominal muscles. The process through which mental states can produce physiological conditions by the way of the autonomic nervous system is well known.

With the proper suggestions a stutterer will not stutter while under hypnosis. As we can duplicate the symptoms of various neuroses under hypnosis, so can we produce the characteristics of stuttering with a non-stutterer. If we give the same subject a post-hypnotic suggestion that he will continue to stutter in his waking state, he will display the same characteristics as a stutterer. Why can't we therefore give the stutterer a post-hypnotic suggestion that he will not stutter in his waking state just as we give the neurotic patient suggestions that he will be free of his symptoms?

Stuttering has often been associated with the feelings of inferiority. In the last analysis, we may consider it as an emotional maladjustment. Stuttering is a symptom of emotional inadequacy. It is the external manifestation of an emotional problem.

It is my contention that the stutterer has given himself negative speech suggestions which makes it impossible for him to speak normally except under certain conditions. He has in effect hypnotized himself and given himself a negative post-hypnotic suggestion. This has been done unconsciously and therefore the stutterer is not aware of it. The proof that he can speak well under certain conditions indicates that with the proper positive suggestions, the stutterer can use perfect speech at all times.

Positive hypnotic suggestions tend to act as a stimulus which travel along the negatively inhibited nerve tract and form a path for proper vocal co-ordination.

Should you desire to contact a qualified speech therapist, I suggest that you write to the Speech Clinic at Wayne University, Detroit, Michigan. They will be able to refer you to an accredited speech therapist in your vicinity through the American Speech and Hearing Association.

INFERIORITY COMPLEX

Use the following suggestions:

"From this moment forth, you will have complete confidence in yourself and in your abilities . . . . You will be more aggressive and outspoken . . . . You no longer will maintain a submissive relationship with people . . . . You will enjoy being with people, and will look forward to meeting new friends and going to social gatherings . . . . You no longer have a fear of people . . . . Moreover, you like people and will find considerable pleasure in mingling with them . . . . You will also banish any fears that you might have had . . . . You will always have perfect self-control and will find that any negative thoughts that you might have felt as to your own abilities or yourself have completely disappeared . . . . YOU NOW HAVE COMPLETE SELF-CONFIDENCE IN YOUR OWN PERSONALITY AND ABILITY . . . . YOU KNOW THAT YOU CAN SUCCEED."

EXCESSIVE SMOKING

These suggestions will prove effective:

"From this moment forth, you will have an intense dislike for cigarettes. The mere taste of a cigarette will make you feel very nauseated and you will be unable to smoke a cigarette . . . . You will refuse all cigarettes offered to you and you will loose your desire for cigarette smoking . . . . Henceforth you will have complete control of your will . . . . You will definitely be able to withstand the temptations of smoking and YOU SHALL NOT SMOKE IN THE FUTURE."

INSOMNIA

Here are suggestions you can use:

"From this moment forth, ~~you~~ will sleep perfectly well every night . . . . The moment ~~you~~ lie down in bed and think of sleeping, ~~you~~ will do so immediately and ~~you~~ will have a sound and restful sleep without awakening until morning.... Moreover, ~~you~~ will not awaken until (Specify time, such as 8 o'clock) in the morning . . . . ~~Your~~ my entire body will benefit immensely from this refreshing slumber . . . .

~~YOU~~ WILL NEVER AGAIN BE TROUBLED WITH INSOMNIA. ~~YOU~~ WILL SLEEP SOUNDLY EVERY NIGHT."

NAIL-BITING

These suggestions should be used:

"From this moment forth you will never again bite your nails . . . . You have beautiful hands and do not want to spoil them by biting your nails . . . . You will not be nervous and your desire to bite your nails will cease immediately. . . . . You will be perfectly content to stop this habit . . . . Moreover, your self-control will be greatly increased and you will definitely be able to withstand the temptation of biting your nails. YOU WILL NEVER AGAIN BITE YOUR FINGERNAILS."

MEMORY TRAINING

You can use these suggestions:

From this moment forth, ~~you~~ will find that ~~your~~ memory will improve tremendously . . . . ~~You~~ will be able to retain impressions very easily and ~~you~~ will readily recall them with a minimum of difficulty . . . . ~~You~~ will find that ~~your~~ memory will have become very keen and that ~~your~~ mind will be a sharper instrument than it has ever been before . . . . When ~~you~~ study, ~~you~~ will find how much easier it is to absorb and remember the contents.

LESSON NINE

The Utility of Suggestion

BY THE UTILIZATION of hypnotism, an actor's or actress' memory can be rendered more retentive. We know that memory becomes very acute under hypnosis, and that facts long forgotten can be easily recalled. This can facilitate the memorization of scripts and also reduce the learning time required.

Hypnotism can be an aid to potential actors who are stage or camera shy because of anticipatory anxiety and whose performances as a consequence are visibly affected by this factor. Many potential stars never achieve success because of this initial barrier. By post-hypnotic suggestion, it is possible to eliminate anxiety, and instill a state of confidence that is soon reflected in the improved quality of their performances. Fatigue resulting from the repeated rehearsals of strenuous scenes can also be greatly reduced. Note newspaper article which follows:

THEATRE HYPNOTIZES ACTORS
TO MAKE 'EM SOUND BETTER

New York—The American theatre will take its first forward step since the introduction of intermission orangeade at the Park Playhouse, Plainfield, N. J., this Thursday night. At that time theatre history will be made. The Playhouse will have its actors hypnotized.

The Plainfield actors will be hypnotized between the first and second acts of "Papa is All." It is confidently predicted that the six Trilbys who play "Papa" will give much better performances in the second act. That's the plan, anyway, and the theatre management is sure it'll work out that way.

It's just an experiment, the management of this barn theatre admits, but the possibilities of the thing are enormous. Anybody can see that it's just a step from hypnotizing actors to putting the hex on critics and the whammy on audiences. If this thing works out right, the time may be at hand when the theatre will have nothing but hits.

The man who'll mesmerize the actors is no carnival fake. He's Dr. Griffith Williams, associate professor of Rutgers University for 16 years and an educator with an academic background of unassailable standing. The Doctor has long been interested in legitimate hypnosis and has already made a successful experiment with the Plainfield actors.

During rehearsals, Dr. Williams hypnotized the six actors while they were still struggling with their lines, made several extra-conscious suggestions, then snapped the actors out of their trance. They learned their lines almost immediately.

"This is no publicity stunt," points out Playhouse publicist Hubert Johnson. "It can't do the theatre any good because this is our last week."

All the actors, says Johnson, volunteered for the experiment and have high hopes that it will increase their acting efficiency. Since Dr. Williams learned his art at Yale, Rochester, the University of Vienna, University of Dijon, and in London, he ought to be able to handle six thespians without too much trouble.

The whole thing opens strange new artistic vistas. Will an actor who is a good actor when under hypnosis and only a fair actor when in his right mind embrace mesmerism as a nightly diet? Will Broadway shows have their own backstage swami for every performance? Will hypnotism eventually replace whiskey and marijuana in our more frenzied musical circles?"

Suppose hypnotism doesn't "take" with some hams? Will Equity allow an actor to be fired because he can't go into a trance? Will certain stars have their own personal Svengalis provided for in their contracts, just as they now demand their personal hairdresser, maid et al?

The idea can be carried even further. Hypnotism can be well used on some box-office crews and on many of our ticket brokers. Surely a hypnotized ticket broker would be an improvement over his normal self.

And just think what a little hypnotism could do in stimulating the imagination of the theatrical press agents.

[87]

Similarly, a person's ability to sing or play a musical instrument can be aided. A person trained in hypnotism will give a better performance than ordinarily because the conscious or subconscious fears that inhibit the display of ability can be controlled by hypnosis. Thus it proves itself an excellent medium in overcoming stage-fright. In the story of Trilby, by George Du Maurier, we recall the wonderful singing voice of Trilby when she is put under hypnosis by Svengali.

Several prominent fighters including a former world light heavyweight have been trained with the aid of hypnotism. Hypnotism gave them increased stamina plus a certain insensibility to their opponent's punches.

Musicians, poets, artists, and writers often create masterpieces while in a state of mind which is closely linked to the light stage of hypnosis. It is well known that such poets as Goethe and Edgar Allen Poe wrote their best works in a state of heightened suggestibility. By using self-hypnosis, Rudyard Kipling clearly visualized the scenes of his colorful narratives, Robert Louis Stevenson did likewise for his most impressive romances, and Richard Wagner received inspiration for his musical masterpieces in the same manner.

Our army administration has found out by actual experience that there are great advantages to be obtained from the use of hypnosis under certain conditions. Spies use self-hypnosis to train their subconscious to record and remember important facts. (See newspaper

[88]

article which follows.) Professional gamblers, by self-hypnosis, can heighten their perception to the point where they can "read" the backs of perfectly honest and unmarked cards by minute variations in manufacture or wear.

SECRECY AIDED BY HYPNOTISM

Los Angeles—Intelligence couriers bearing secret messages need not rely on invisible ink, or tissue paper pellets under their fingernails, to thwart enemy agents.

They literally lock their secrets in their heads so that no amount of torture could wrest it from them.

"Let us say that an intelligence officer is carrying a vital message from General Clay in Germany to Secretary Marshall in Washington.

"The officer is hypnotized. While he is under the trance, you read the message to him. After it has been 'implanted' in his mind, you tell him that he is to repeat it only if he is greeted with the words. 'How are you? You look mighty, mighty well.' Otherwise he is not to remember a thing.

"Those words of greeting, or any others you care to agree upon, are what we call a 'trigger.' They touch off the messenger's subconscious memory, so that when you say them to him, he automatically and involuntarily delivers the message out loud.

THE UTILITY OF SUGGESTION

"If espionage agents from another power were to capture the messenger, they could never learn the secret, even if they tortured him or gave him the truth serum for the simple reason that the messenger himself does not know what it is unless the trigger words are said to him."

All successful salesmen know how to influence others and get the interest of their prospective customers even though they may never have heard of hypnotism nor have the slightest idea of what it means. If you confront them with the fact that they have used the same techniques that are commonly employed in hypnotism they would be very surprised indeed, but the fact is that they have done so. The getting and keeping of the subject's attention; the use of emotional appeal; the fixing of his gaze on yours; the maintainance of a serene and self-confident approach and various other techniques are all hypnotic procedures. Many successful people actually know how to "charm" and influence their acquaintances. In many instances this is done subconsciously.

The principles of suggestion can be beneficial to every salesman or potential salesman. In a sense we are all salesmen for we do sell our services. A suggestion is an idea or emotion which acts on the mind as a stimulus to promote action. The salesman's job is to present these ideas and emotions to the prospective customer in such a way as to involve the least resistance. Sell your product or service solely on its merit. Speak to the prospective customer in terms of his own advantage.

Use the power of suggestion cleverly, and you will prove yourself to be an expert salesman.

I went to one of the department stores to buy some shirts that were advertised in the newspaper. This sale was actually made before I reached the store. The salesman needed only to show me the shirts. As I was leaving, the salesman said to me, "You don't need any ties, do you? He suggested to me that I didn't need any ties. Wasn't that a bad approach? If he had said, "I have some beautiful silk ties that would match your shirts, I'd like to show you some," my curiosity would have been aroused. I would have extended him the courtesy of looking at the ties, and probably would have purchased several.

Rule No. 1 is: Never offer a customer a negative suggestion. If you say that an article is pretty, do not stop there. Continue to point out why you think it is pretty and why it is a good buy.

An executive of one of the largest chain drug stores in California, who had taken our course, increased the sale of cigarettes tremendously in his drug stores by the utilization of this power of suggestion. He inaugurated the practice of having the cashier say to every customer, "Cigarettes?" Her voice being warm and pleasant was responsible for many sales that would ordinarily not have been made. This practice is now compulsory in all his drugstores in the Western division.

Successful sales executives realize the full importance of suggestion as a psychological approach to the selling problem. If possible, exhibit your product. Use charts and pictures. Allow the prospect to handle the product. It invites sales. Isn't it difficult for a woman to resist a new hat after she has tried it on and likes it? She may have a dozen hats at home, but suddenly she forgets about them and feels that she must have this new hat. The "clincher" in selling an automobile is to let the customer take the car for a road test "behind the wheel." Let him get the "feel" of it. If you are selling a man with a family an insurance policy, do not begin by talking about the price of insurance. Emphasize the benefits to the man's wife and his children. Begin in a positive manner.

By auto-suggestion or self-hypnosis you can implant positive and dynamic suggestions in your mind just as the hypochondriac implants negative suggestions. Auto-suggestion is a wonderful science if you cultivate it.

Feel that you are going to succeed in life and in business. The reason that some men fail in business is that they approach it with a negative attitude. There are many examples of this in your own community.

The successful man knew before he started that he would be successful; he had the conviction, the courage, and confidence that he was going to make the grade, and so he did. Is this not auto-suggestion? "As a man thinketh, so is he."

The salesman must have the conviction and confidence that he is going to sell. If he thinks success, he will be successful. If he leaves his home in the morning and says to himself, "I know I'm not going to make any sales today, but I'll see the customers just the same," the probability is that he will not make a single sale. If, on the other hand, the salesman leaves his house, knowing that he will overcome any obstacles that he may encounter, the probability of increased sales are so much greater.

You must possess personal attraction or charm to succeed. In order to sell your product or services, the customer usually must be sold on you. To win friends, we must exert a positive influence. Why is it that we seek the companionship and friendship of certain individuals? Why is it that after leaving certain people we continue on our way in better spirits, while others may leave us in a depressed mood? To cultivate personal attraction, study those who please you. Discover what elements in their personality make them attractive.

There is no "magic" in the art of successful living. Self-confidence, positive attitudes, personal magnetism, and happiness are attained through the application of positive and specific principles of constructive thinking that are "suggested" to the subconscious mind through the medium of hypnotism. It is therefore the hypnotist and his medium, hypnotism, which is the "key" not only to the release of this wonderful "Life Force," but also to the direction of that force for better living, success, and ultimate recognition in our highly competitive society.

LESSON TEN

The Universality of Hypnotism

THE FOLLOWING ARTICLES are excerpts from various newspapers that will prove of interest to students of hypnotism:

HYPNOTISM COURSE NOW AVAILABLE TO PUBLIC

Hypnotism is fast coming into its own. At one time its mention aroused mixed feelings of fascination and fear. Now, the fascination remains, but familiarity with the usages of hypnotism has helped remove the fear.

"Informed minds everywhere accept hypnotism as an aid in better living," is the opinion held by Melvin Powers, and it is conceded by some authorities that by means of it, one can strengthen his memory, his mind, and his will.

"Basically, hypnotism is an efficient tool for contacting the subconscious mind," said Mr. Powers, "and is largely used by psychiatrists today in veteran rehabilitation in accomplishing their miraculous cures." Mr. Powers is the founder of The American Society for Advancement of Hypnosis and author of the books, "Hypnotism Revealed," "Advanced Techniques of Hypnosis," "Mental Power Through Sleep Suggestion," "Dynamic Thinking" and "Self-Hypnosis." He has been conducting classes for doctors in techniques of hypnosis. However popular demand from the people who look to hypnotism as an aid developing talent, memory and personality, has induced Mr. Powers to extend the course to the laity.

"Everyone can learn to hypnotize himself for his own good," says Mr. Powers, director of the school, which by the way is the only school of its kind on the West Coast.—**Hollywood Register.**

HYPNOTIST CLASSES IN HOLLYWOOD
NOW IN NINTH YEAR

Melvin Powers, a professional hypnotist, has been conducting classes in hypnotism, self-hypnosis and psychiatry for the last eight years in this city. The complete curriculum is divided into two component parts; the introductory course and the advanced course. The introductory course provides a comprehensive study of the science of hypnotism, self-hypnosis, and abnormal psychology. Here the students, who average twelve to a class, analyze and discuss clearly and thoroughly the basic principles governing hypnotism, hypno-analysis and psycho-analysis.

[94]

The students also learn self-hypnosis to overcome such conditions as insomnia, nail-biting, smoking, excessive drinking, and stage-fright.

The advanced course is designed for those persons who wish to advance their study in personality disorders and in the principles and practices of psychiatry and psychoanalysis. It presents in an organized manner the essential knowledge of modern psychology and mental hygiene. The requirements for admission for the Powers course are a deep interest in psychology and personal improvement.—**Los Angeles News.**

USE HYPNOSIS ON MOTHER AS BABY IS BORN

Baltimore.—A 22-year-old nurse gave birth to a 7 pound 10 ounce boy at Johns Hopkins Hospital yesterday under the hypnotic influence of a psychiatrist. The infant was her first. Her physician was Dr. Harold Rosen, a member of the hospital's psychiatric department. An obstetrician was in attendance, but did nothing. It was the hospital's first hypnotic birth.

The patient had her baby within three hours after entering the hospital. She remained conscious throughout the time she spent in the delivery room.

Dr. George Anderson, obstetrician, stood by while Dr. Rosen hypnotized her. Hospital authorities said she had suggested the method herself after consultation with both physicians.

Dr. Anderson said later that the delivery "went very well." But he cautioned that medical conclusions could not be drawn from a single case.

"Hypnosis is only one of a number of agents and procedures that can be used in obstetrics to lessen pain and anxiety," said Dr. Rosen, "It should be carefully limited to suitable cases."

The patient, who showed no sign of any pain during birth, and her baby apparently were doing fine.

HYPNOTISM BY PHONE AS BIRTH
ANAESTHESIA TOLD

Los Angeles—In the maternity ward of a Chicago hospital a young wife about to undergo the labor of childbirth, receives a long-distance telephone call from Los Angeles. Her nervous tension relaxes as she recognizes the reassuring voice:

"This is Dr. Kroger. I shall count three. You will then fall asleep. Your labor will be entirely painless . . . falling . . . asleep."

This unusual scene probably will be enacted twice during the next few days. It will be the first time in medical history that hypnotic anaesthesia has been administered by long-distance telephone.

[95]

THE UNIVERSALITY OF HYPNOTISM

Dr. William S. Kroger, noted Chicago physician and former faculty member of the University of Illinois Medical School, has just arrived in Los Angeles to lecture at Southern California hospitals. Two of his women patients in Chicago are very close to the time of accouchement.

If this happens before his return, Dr. Kroger said today, he would hypnotize them by wire. He has hypnotized patients frequently by telephone within the limits of Chicago but never before attempted the long-distance method.

Delivers 23 Babies

Dr. Kroger has delivered 23 babies painlessly by hypnotism. Pain in childbirth, he remarked, is absent among primitive peoples and is magnified by fear among the civilized.

DENTISTS FIND HYPNOTIC SLEEP SURE ANESTHETIC

Fargo, N. D.—Seven North Dakota dentists are successfully using psychosomatic sleep, generally known as hypnosis, as an anesthetic, leaving patients with no discomfort or pain.

The technique was reported 97 percent effective in trials on 250 patients. The "suggestive anesthesia" was developed with the aid of Dr. Thomas R. Burgess, director of the psychology department of Concordia College, Moorhead, Minn.

In their first report on the development, the dentists made these major points:

Psychosomatic sleep is safe and will in no way affect a patient's mind, character or general health; a patient cannot be placed into the sleep against his will, nor can he be made to violate his moral, religious or ethical code of life; a subject has complete control of his own well-being while in the trance, will always awake from it on an order from the operator or at a time previously set by the operator, and the operator need not be present at the awakening hour.

The dentists made their findings public at a meeting of the southeastern district of the North Dakota Dental Society. They said only 11 of the 250 patients failed to go into trances at first sittings. Four of these were put asleep in later sessions. Subsequently, four more of the 11 were placed into deep sleep but were unable to produce anesthesia. The remaining trio were complete failures.

The practitioners said every type of dental operation was performed.

HYPNOTISM REVEALED

FINDS HYPNOTISM AID TO DENTAL EXTRACTIONS

Bakersfield, Calif.—Hypnotism, long thought of as a good stage trick and now used in medicine and in curing mental ills, has found a happy place in dentistry here.

A patient went to Hendrick's Medical Dental Clinic. She had two teeth that had to come out and she was allergic to all types of anesthetic.

Dr. Neil Norton, consulting psycho-therapist, and two other doctors were called for consultation by Dr. Meredith Hendricks, who was to remove the teeth. Norton began talking to the patient. Within a few seconds she was in a hypnotic trance.

Thirty minutes later she was brought out of it, her two teeth pulled but completely unaware that they were gone. Though the doctors and two other witnesses told her the operation was over, a mirror was the only thing that convinced her.

Dr. W. G. Hendricks, a brother of the doctor who performed the operation, reported the patient suffered no ill after-effects such as bleeding, swelling or shocks.

MEMORY OF 20 YEARS RESTORED

New Rochelle, New York—A 29 year old housewife, the first 20 years of her life blacked out by amnesia, recalled her girlhood today after psychiatrist using hypnosis helped lift the curtain that had obscured her for that long period of time. She had lost all memory of her existence in Braddock, Pennsylvania, neither remembering her family or friends. She thought she was an orphan, not realizing that she had disappeared from the Pennsylvania town nine years ago.

Under hypnosis, she disclosed details that had been long lost to her conscious mind. She found when she awoke that the dreams and fantasies of her hidden past had taken on realistic patterns and form.

She told her doctor that the last day she could remember was in 1942 when she found herself walking dazedly, along a highway near Latrobe, Pennsylvania. Unable to remember her name or her home, she obtained a job as a waitress and later met her future husband in New Rochelle. Today she and her husband are still amazed at her recovery. The headaches and nervous tensions that she previously had are gone and the days of her youth are all clear.

While she was under hypnosis, Dr. Selby went over the names of towns in Pennsylvania until he reached "Braddock." This name created a response in the patient. He got in touch with authorities there and learned that a woman fitting her description had disappeared in 1940 and had been sought in vain.

In the next treatment at his office, Dr. Selby hypnotized his patient and began to talk about her family in Braddock. She remembered the persons and events. Then the psychiatrist commanded her to retain that memory and broke the hypnotic spell. It worked successfully.

[97]

THE UNIVERSALITY OF HYPNOTISM

The following article appeared in the February 7, 1955 issue
of TIME.

HYPNOSIS FOR BURNS

All the standard methods of treatment had failed. Like many
severe-burn victims, a group of patients at Dallas' Parkland Hospital morosely refused to eat or to exercise, cried out for narcotics,
and suffered from skin grafts that would not heal. For lack of
nutrition, the men's wounds were getting worse instead of better.
Then a five-man team from the University of Texas' Southwestern Medical School decided to try an age-old, much-debated therapeutic gimmick—hypnosis.

The treatment was repeated daily, directed at specific problems.
Sample hypnotic formulas: "When you wake up, the area in which
you have been burned will not be painful in any sense of the word.
It is not going to hurt you, but you must be careful not to injure
it," or "When you wake up, you are going to be hungry. You are
going to want tuna fish and milk and meat and butter. The right
food will help make you well again." So far, hypnosis has brought
six difficult test cases around. Among them:

¶ B. W., 24, with second-degree burns covering 45% of his body
surface, had undergone several unsuccessful skin grafts in 18
months, went from 130 to 90 lbs. because of refusal to eat properly. Skin infections and contractures (contracted-burn scar tissue) made it difficult for him to move his limbs and neck. Within
a few days after hypnosis began, he was taking 4,200 calories per
day, became cheerful and cooperative. Thanks to improved diet,
skin grafts began to "take." Twelve weeks later, B. W., healed,
walked out of the hospital.

¶ J. C., 33, suffered 45% body-surface burns in a boiler explosion.
His dressings could only be changed under anesthesia; he feared
moving his painfully burned hands and fingers. The Southwestern
team started daily hypnosis; shunning narcotics, the patient obe-
diently began to exercise his hands as instructed every 30 minutes,
even in his sleep, until the doctors stopped him with a post-
hypnotic order.

¶ C. J., 32, suffered from 35% burns, started hypnotic treatment
only four hours after the injury. As a result, no anesthesia was
required to dull pain, even during skin grafts. With a good appetite and exercise, C. J. spent only 18 days in hospital.

Last week, coached by psychologist Harold Crasilneck, the Southwestern team was using hypnosis on yet another patient: a 29-
year old victim of Buerger's disease, a circulatory ailment heavily
aggravated by smoking. After hypnosis, the patient refused to
touch cigarettes, retched when one was offered. Result: steady
improvement. The team hopes to extend the technique to other
chronic ailments, but, warns Crasilneck: "As we see it now, hypnosis has a very definite, specific role in medicine. We don't for
a moment say it is a cure-all."

"Courtesy TIME; copyright Time Inc. 1955."

HYPNOTISM REVEALED

A SENSATIONAL REPORT
LONDON,---APRIL 1955

Hypnotism, the uncanny power of one mind over another, becomes respectable as from now. It is officially accepted as a most effective form of treatment by the British medical profession.

A report recommending the fullest use of hypnotism wherever it can help has been sent today to more than 60,000 doctors by the British Medical Association.

It is based on an 18-month inquiry by experts led by Professor T. Ferguson Rodger, of Glasgow University, who have examined the claims of medical hypnotists and studied their methods.

The experts state they are convinced that hypnotism really has the power to help sick people and relieve pain.

For thousands suffering from "psychosomatic" ailments—disorders with real symptoms but imaginary causes — hypnosis may be the best treatment available, the report to the doctors states.

Such symptoms include stubborn skin inflammation brought on by "nerves," palpitations of an otherwise healthy heart, headaches and body pains for which no organic causes exists.

The report endorses the use of hypnotism for helping to relieve the pain of childbirth and occasionally to replace anaesthetics in operations.

It may also be the best treatment for certain forms of neurosis, enabling the doctor to detect the hidden mental conflicts at the root of the disorder.

"As a method of treatment, hypnotism has proved its ability to remove symptoms and alter morbid habits of thought and behaviour," says the report.

SO QUICK

Yesterday the four experts—Professor Rodger, Professor Alexander Kennedy, of Edinburgh, Dr. Edward Bennet, of London's Institute of Psychiatry, and Dr. Steuart Noy Scott, a physician —commented on their hypnosis inquiry, the first to be carried out by the B.M.A. for 60 years.

They pointed out at a conference that hypnotism often benefits a patient so quickly that it may eventually become one of the main answers to the serious overcrowding of the mental hospitals.

"Because of the relative brevity of treatment with hypnotism, research may contribute to a solution of the problem created by the very large number of people requiring psycho - therapy (treatment by psychological means)," they said.

THE UNIVERSALITY OF HYPNOTISM

ANYONE

The experts are so convinced of hypnotism's value that they urge all hospitals to teach the art of it to medical students.

Hypnotism is an art which almost anyone can learn, the experts stressed. It is not an inborn gift peculiar to a few "Svengali" types.

So not only psychiatrists but family doctors may now make use of a black magic device which has been professionally discredited for centuries.

The precise methods of inducing hypnosis, which involve such devices as watching flashing lights and listening to monotonously repeated words, are withheld from the report.

(Nobody knows how hypnotism works, except that it seems to lull the critical faculties of the mind which would normally resent the commands of the hypnotist.

Some specially susceptible people can be put into a trance at the hypnotist's first attempt, but with most people several sessions are needed.

There is no shut-down of brain activity and no suspension of consciousness during hypnosis as there is during sleep. Brain-wave recordings made under hypnosis are like those of a wakeful person.)

The experts could only define hypnosis vaguely by calling it a "state of altered attention induced by another person."

During this state strange changes may appear, such as immunity to pain, temporary paralysis, and extreme susceptibility to carry out suggestions made by the hypnotist.

Though hypnotism will never be a cure-all, its ultimate value may be so great that the experts recommend a full-scale program of research to probe its precise effects on the brain and mind. The Medical Research Council may now be asked to sponsor such experiments.

At the same time, scientists should look for a possible link between hypnotism and faith cures, the experts suggest.

"Hypnotism was known and used as a means of healing mainly in a religious setting by the major ancient civilizations," the report states.

It now takes its place among the synthetic drugs, electric machines, and gleaming instruments of the modern clinic.

HYPNOSIS IN MEDICINE

by A. PHILIP MAGONET, M. D.

President Medical Hypnosis Association

This book is the fruit of many years experience with several thousand patients in using hypnosis. It was written to encourage doctors and students of hypnosis to further explore the field of hypnosis. I have listed below the entire contents of this excellent book to give you a complete picture of the nature of the material contained in it. I most certainly would advise your reading it and I am sure that you will be proud to add this book to your collection of hypnotic books.

Contents are as follows:

104 Pages $1

Advanced Techniques of Hypnosis

(Photographically Illustrated)

by Melvin Powers

Hypnosis is primarily a technical means of helping those who are in distress because of subjective fears or pressures of whatever kind, be they of a mental, spiritual, or physical nature. It is with this serious purpose, and with the scientific implementation of hypnosis, that we are concerned in this book.

There have been many books written on the therapeutic value of hypnosis. Numerous volumes have dealt with its history, and many more have been concerned with its various phenomena. There has, however, been comparatively little written about the actual technique of inducing the hypnotic state. Since this phase of hypnosis has been so woefully neglected, we have not had the rapid technical development our vital science so rightfully deserves. This volume is designed to remedy that lack.

I have personally known psychologists who had given up using hypnosis solely because of the inability to effect the hypnotic state in their patients, but who, when at last were properly shown how easily this state could be induced in most subjects, were finally unanimous in their enthusiastic acceptance of its therapeutic value.

This book is dedicated to those who aspire to a fuller understanding of hypnotic procedures. It is my purpose to show you, the reader, how to develop any individual into a receptive hypnotic subject, and to give you the necessary understanding and knowledge required to achieve this end. You will also be instructed in the use of my original techniques, which have proven to be so wonderfully effective in my long experience as a professional hypnotist. A careful reading of the book will not only be rewarding because of the wealth of information contained in it, but will also assure the reader maximum professional efficiency in the exciting, and fascinating practice of advanced hypnosis.

"Instantaneous Hypnosis"

One of the most interesting aspects of hypnosis is the phenomenon of "Instantaneous Hypnosis." I have been requested to divulge the mystery of this phenomenon on numerous occasions. When I answer that there is no mystery in this procedure at all, but that it comes about soley through the skillful application of psychology, I am met with incredulous stares. The fact of the matter is, nevertheless, that the operation is quite simple, and requires but an understanding of applied psychology, and skill in the manipulation of hypnotic suggestion. "Instantaneous Hypnosis" is indeed, a sensational, but nevertheless sound, hypnotic phenomenon. You will be shown how you can accomplish this.

"Stage Hypnotism"

The Stage Hypnotist has always been a source of keen interest to the public and has frequently fired its imagination with his sensational showmanship. While the stage hypnotist's activities do seem to be histrionic and magical to the uninitiated, the students of the subject know very well that his procedure is extremely scientific and carefully calculated to gain his ends. We will sit in on a session in which the stage hypnotist is already at work, and notice how scientific his approach really is.

"Waking Hypnosis"

We are all affected by the irresistible influence of suggestion. We merely vary in the degree to which we respond to it. By systematic suggestions, multitudes can be made through propaganda to act as a unit, even though there had been no previous attachment to the ideas communicated. Under the stress of emotional stimuli, we are lead easily to commit acts that we normally would never dream of perpetrating. This effect is most notably achieved through the irresistible force of suggestion rationalized under the most properly prepared conditions for their greatest effect.

Chapter titles are as follows:

128 PAGES — $1

Sleep and Learn

MENTAL THERAPY AND MIND-TRAINING WHILE YOU SLEEP

THERE is abundant scientific evidence demonstrating that the subconscious, without a doubt, functions while we sleep. We know further that dreams originate in the subconscious. During sleep we continue to breathe and digest our food, while the other processes of the body also operate without our awareness. Although we roll to the edge of the bed, we rarely roll out of it because our subconscious mind protects us from doing so. To become uncovered during the night does not necessitate our awakening because we mechanically correct this condition while we continue to sleep. A mother may be able to sleep through the heaviest thunderstorms and blissfully dream through the loudest noises of her husband's breathing, but the moment her baby stirs in his crib, her subconscious mind is immediately alerted and she finds herself wide awake. These facts are clear evidence that the subconscious is constantly functioning and that it steadily is receiving suggestions even during the so called unawareness of deep sleep. In hypnosis, our purpose is to convey suggestions to the subconscious mind. Sleep-suggestion is another remarkably efficient way of achieving this.

A method has been devised that now makes it possible to use the restful hours of sleep for purposes of mental therapy and study. This is done through the use of records. A clock controlled phonograph which can be set to play one record or series of them is used for this purpose. The phonograph which can be set to play at intervals for any length of time is automatic and shuts itself off when its assigned task is finished. To insure complete privacy, a pillow-speaker is placed beneath the pillow during the night so that the record transmits solely to the person for whom it is intended. In this manner, suggestions or information are softly communicated to the subconscious mind in an effortless and restful way without awakening the sleeper or disturbing any other occupant of the room.

Since the mind is very receptive to suggestion during hypnosis, sleep, and periods of relaxation, because mental stress under these conditions is at a minimum, much can be done to influence its operation.

By transmitting knowledge to the subconscious mind through this process of mechanized sleep-suggestion many arduous years can be cut from the educational process. The greatest advantage of sleep-learning is that it eliminates such constantly irritating difficulties as the conscious inability to concentrate while learning. A third of our lives is spent in sleeping. Why should we not profitably employ this valuable time for therapy or study? Such subjects as mathematics, music, and languages can be learned with ease during the hours of sleep and in such a wonderfully easy manner too, through the use of these record suggestions.

The following experiment in sleep-learning was conducted at the University of North Carolina under the direction of Professor Charles R. Elliott. Forty students, all with perfect hearing, were picked for this test case. The group was divided into two sections of twenty students. Each group slept in Professor Elliott's psychological laboratory for three hours. Electroencephalographs were used to test the condition and depth of each student's slumber. One section slept undisturbed, while the other twenty were exposed to a recording containing a list of words which was piped to each individually through the medium of pillow speakers.

When all the students were awakened, they were asked to memorize this list. Those who had heard it previously learned it with incredible rapidity. The others labored falteringly to attain the same end. Professor Elliott concluded therefore that the process of sleep-teaching was similar to that of reteaching material that had once been known and temporarily forgotten.

Information such as multiplication tables, chemical formulas, the Morse code, logarithms, vocabularies, languages, and other subjects can be easily taught through sleep-education. In teaching the Morse code, the Army and Navy have used sleep-education with the most phenomenal results. The men literally slept their way to successful achievement in this highly technical field! What a wonderful aid this medium is for those who have poor memories too. Learning is not only made easy but permanent because of the receptive condition under which this learning takes place.

The following article appeared in the April, 1949 issue of Musical America.

LEARNED OPERA WHILE ASLEEP, MET STAR REVEALS

The singer in question, it appears, is Ramon Vinay, who mastered the Italian text of the role of Don Jose, in Carmen, for his first performance of it at La Scala in Milan, in two weeks' time by use of a special type of phonograph which enabled him to perform this prodigious feat of memorization largely while asleep at night.

On the theory that soft-voiced repetition of the lesson to be learned provides the most effortless and effective means of committing it to memory, the phonograph transmits through an under-the-pillow speaker sound which can be heard only by the sleeper, who, with his conscious mind completely relaxed, is able to learn more quickly than he would be while awake and without any evidence of fatigue.

The machine contains a clock that can be preset, with quarter-hour controls, to start and stop the records automatically. Mr. Vinay did not play the records all night long. He used them for half an hour while dropping off to sleep and for an half hour before waking time in the morning.

The new learning device opens endless vistas. Mr. Vinay plans to learn the role of Tristan by means of it, in time for the fall season at La Scala.

———————

The sleep-o-matic phonograph is also an excellent means of bringing about improvement in the psychological and psycho-somatic fields. Persons with complexes, anxieties, and fears can obtain great benefit from this new medium of correction which can eliminate these conditions which persist because the individual has become the victim of negative suggestions or stimuli which hang on tenaciously. We have already mentioned the fact that the subconscious is susceptible to suggestion and that it is constantly receiving impressions, stimuli, and suggestions of varying kinds, which are mentally recorded and later acted upon. It is primarily negative suggestions; however, that cause the emotional problems of the individual.

Positive, constructive suggestions repeated to the subconscious during hypnosis or sleep can cancel or recondition any negative attitudes that harass the individual. Positive personality changes create a constructive and happier outlook; however, this is a complex problem and requires close personal attention. The psychodynamics of the problem must be clearly understood and demand conscious control and understanding.

The sleep-o-matic phonograph can be used successfully with children to eliminate such undesirable habits as nail-biting, thumb-sucking, bed-wetting, and unruliness. Their personality problems can also be treated very easily and efficiently through the use of recorded suggestions that can direct and influence their subconscious minds. A mother could through the use of these effective recordings give healthful orientation to her children in a painless and pleasant manner.

It is not an exaggeration to say that the sleep-o-matic recordings could be of inestimable value in the correction of personality problems that lead to juvenile delinquency. It is not; however, our purpose to maintain that these recordings alone could solve the problems of delinquency, but that they would be an invaluable aid in the social reorientation of confused junior citizens.

The principle of giving suggestions to those asleep is by no means new. The "sleep temples" of ancient Egypt were sanctuaries where people went to receive the benefits of helpful suggestions on matters of health and living while they slept. It is only recently, however, that any serious work has been done in this field. The possibilities of self-improvement through its use are unlimited. We are undoubtedly entering an era of new insights and understanding which may open new vistas of human achievement in the future. This is a most effective instrument for the creation of good habit patterns. It can be used in the establishment of new learning processes, for the relief of nervous tension, the attainment of complete relaxation, for peace of mind, the re-creation of energy, the reclamation of confidence, and even instill an added zest for living. Latent talent, ambition, and enthusiasm can be reclaimed from the dark recesses of the subconscious through the dynamic suggestions of the sleep-o-matic phonographic recordings. It is possible through these recordings to become a more dynamic, confident, and inspired human being!

We are all aware that success in life is dependent upon one's state of mind and how one uses one's creative abilities. One must marshall one's thoughts to create a new philosophy that will help one live with equanimity and fortitude. The road to happiness, peace of mind, success, and abundance requires persistance, patience, imagination, and faith. These worthy ends can be achieved through the proper use of our sleep-o-matic phonograph. It can be the best counselor and teacher anyone ever had!

As we have mentioned in the foregoing, the subconscious mind can be influenced through sleep-suggestion. This access to the subconscious can be used as a means to attain desired ends that we could not achieve through the ordinary processes of communication. Once we understand the immense potential and significance of the subconscious mind in our daily lives, we will be able to use that knowledge for a better integration of our personal resources for a brighter future.

Does this sound roseate? I feel my enthusiasm is justified. Has this not all been done before and effectively too through hypnosis? Yes, much has been accomplished and much more will be accomplished with this wonderful phonograph. Psychological and medical books are filled with case histories proving the tremendous power of suggestion. It is my belief that the sleep-o-matic phonograph and sleep-o-matic tape recorder are the best means yet known for the transference of suggestion when hypnosis is not available.

I have discussed a new and sensational method of bringing helpful suggestions to everyone. Each individual can make his own recorded suggestions and use them accordingly for his personal needs. The efficacy of this method has already been proven by outstanding authorities. A brighter, happier, and richer life can be yours. Live and learn! Sleep and learn! Let sleep which regenerates your body, improve the power of your mind. I have written a thought provoking and inspirational book based on using the period of sleep for self-improvement, therapy, and learning. It is titled, *Mental-Power Through Sleep-Suggestion* and is described on the back cover. I sincerely recommend this book to those who are further interested in learning about this marvelous, fascinating science. An illustrated catalog of sleep-o-matic units, records, and accessories will be sent to you. You will also be shown how your own phonograph or tape recorder can easily be used for this purpose.

SLEEP AND LEARN

The following article appeared in the June 18, 1950 edition of the Los Angeles Times:

MENTAL SUGGESTION MAY
HELP FAT-REDUCING DIET

By Lydia Lane

"Don't let people get away with the excuse that glandular trouble causes their being fat," declares a university doctor and professor, "because 99.44% of them are fat because they eat too much."

The obesity, he explained, was caused for the most part by an over-emphasis on starchy foods. But why do people overeat? Psychiatrists tell us that an abnormal appetite does not necessarily imply an excessive love of food but often is the result of emotional disturbance. What to do about this craving for food, especially in those who are not happy, becomes a real problem.

Group Effort Suggested

A solution suggested by a recent Public Health conference was the formation of a reducing group known as "Appetites Anonymous" to be patterned after the famous "Alcoholics Anonymous."

When overeating is a habit of long standing, it becomes increasingly difficult to diet. The desire to be thin is not as great as the desire to eat, so these poor unfortunates start reducing but soon break their resolutions.

Record Devised

An interesting and effective way to solve this problem is to receive constructive suggestion during sleep. There is a machine especially designed with a pillow speaker to train the subconscious mind at night.

This painless method re-educates and reconditions habits so that after sleeping over a record which suggests that you no longer have an abnormal appetite, you find yourself with unbelievable power to resist what at one time seemed irresistible.

Action Intermittent

This machine plays records which train your subconscious mind during sleep and is constructed so that it will go on and off at specified intervals.

If you have a problem of insomnia, nervousness or reducing and would like to try this method, it is possible to rent a machine at a nominal figure.

[111]

SLEEP AND LEARN

The following article appeared in the October 16, 1950 issue of TIME.

NEW HELDENTENOR

Burly Tenor Ramon (Otello) Vinay was in a sweat. A Chilean trained for Italian and French opera, he had worked hard for over a year to huff himself into a German-style **Heldentenor,** and he was all set to sing his first Tristan, with Kirsten Flagstad as Isolde. San Franciscans (and Metropolitan Opera General Manager Rudolf Bing, who sorely needs a successor to Lauritz Melchior) were all set to hear him. But a fortnight ago, with debut day almost at hand, Tenor Vinay was bogged down in Chile. A stubborn Santiago de Chile impresario refused to let him leave the country until he fulfilled a delayed engagement. Last week, finally freed by persuasion and compromise, Vinay flew to San Francisco, took his big step, was cheered by audience and critics.

He had rushed in two days late, hurried through two piano rehearsals and one with orchestra. He was not worried about his own role of Tristan—although he had found Wagnerian themes "strange for the Latin ear." HE HAD HELPED HIMSELF TO MEMORIZE HIS ROLE BY SLEEPING WITH THE SPEAKER OF A CEREBROGRAPH (AUTOMATIC RECORD PLAYER) UNDER HIS PILLOW TO EMBED THE MUSIC IN HIS SUBCONSCIOUS. But, not knowing German itself, he expected to have a dreadful time following the other singers and catching his cues. Flagstad ("She was always there prompting me or giving me a signal with her eyes") took care of that.

On the big night, the audience in San Francisco's opera house found huge (6 ft. 2 in., 220 lbs.) and handsome Tenor Vinay visually, if not vocally, a heroic match for Soprano Kirsten Flagstad. Wrote San Francisco Chronicle Critic Alfred Frankenstein: "To be sure, [Vinay] did not bring the music all the suppleness and vocal ease one hoped for, but he brought it something else that was almost equally important—a tenderness, lyricism and fragility of expression that were altogether unprecedented. For once, Tristan's ravings in the third act seemed only five times too long instead of ten or twenty or a hundred." Vinay's phrasing, particularly when set off against Flagstad's magnificent subtlety, seemed more memorized than inspired. But that defect might well disappear with time.

"Courtesy of TIME, Copyright Time Inc., 1950"